Sinead O'connor Autobiography

MOIRA BOWEN

Contents

MOIRA BOWEN	1
Part One	5
Hey hey, we're the Monkees!	6
The piano	7
lourdes	15
my aunt francis	21
The train	22
lost in the music	28
My mother's record collection	39
The house of the rising sun, part one	46
The house of the rising sun, part two	52
The house of the rising sun, part three	59
I sing to the siren	68
sisters	74
any dream will do	79
Juan, i love you	81
about my dad	83
poem of my youth	86
The second part	87
Who are you?	88
settling in	104
a lesson or two	109
flammable matter	116
shave my head	120

The lion and the cobra	124
clocks and woks	129
My Boy Lollipop, July 1987	136
The way young lovers do	143
There is a light and it never goes out, 1987	146
WHAT IS THE GOOD NEWS? WHAT IS THE BAD NEWS?	156
ROSES MADE OF PAPER	162
SHEVITI ADONAI L'NEGDI TAMID (In Hebrew:)	164
SATURDAY NIGHT LIVE, PART ONE OF WAR, 1992	184
It's not necessarily so	198
MY BANNER OF THE STARS	208
Part three	214
some musical notes	215
IS IT TRUE THAT I'M YOUR GIRL?	222
MOTHER OF THE UNIVERSE	224
gospel oak	234
faith and courage	238
Sean-Nós Nua	241
Throw down your arms	243
Theology	246
What if it's me?	249
I'm not bossy	253
Coming soon . . .	255
dagger through my heart	259

The greatest love of all 260
lou reed 268
Some lessons and real stories 270
mr big things 272
Jake, Roisin, Shane and Yeshua 274
The Wizard of Oz 287
forward and now 299

PART ONE

HEY HEY, WE'RE THE MONKEES!

Here is the structure of my family and who I was with when before you start.

My mother, Marie, and father, John, wed in 1960 and settled in Crumlin, Dublin, the neighborhood where they were raised. After the birth of my brother Joe three years later, they relocated to middle-class Glenageary, which was located on the opposite side of the city. My sister Éimear then arrived in 1965. 14 months later, in 1966, I followed. After that, my brother John in 1968.

My father made the wise decision to desert my mother in 1975, and this book will explain why. When he was granted custody of us, my (adorable) stepmom Viola and I moved in with him and his new partner. But because we missed our mother, my younger brother and I only stayed for around six months.

I was nine years old at the time. After living with my mother until I was thirteen years old, I voluntarily moved back in with my father. After what had been occurring at my mother's house, I was unable to adjust, so around the end of my thirteenth year, I entered what is formally referred to as a "rehabilitation center for girls with behavior problems." (I believe everyone is aware that my dad is entitled to a reimbursement for that since it obviously did not work.)

I left the center when I was fifteen and enrolled in a residential school in Waterford. That summer, I joined a band, and when school started again, I missed the band. To the sorrow of my dear father, I therefore ran away from school in December when I became sixteen and rented a studio or room. After I consented to have the nose piercing he had already performed for me removed, he finally agreed to let me stay. He paid my rent, but he didn't pay any of my other expenditures, so I had to get a job. He is brilliant.

Viola, my father's second wife, has three daughters from a previous union. My stepsisters are three, therefore. Eoin is another son that Viola and my father share. He is therefore also my brother.

My mother was killed in a vehicle accident in 1985. I was 18 years old at the time. I traveled to London later that year after accepting Ensign Records' invitation to sign a contract with them.

When I was twenty, three weeks before the release of my debut record, I gave birth to my first kid. I also have three other kids and two grandchildren so far.

THE PIANO

We are spending christmas at the home of my paternal grandmother, which—the house, not her—usually always smells like cabbage.

The other lights below are off because they are only on around the tree. With their backs to the chamber and hurrying up and down the stairs out of concern for one another, the adults are in the blue shadow. I'm small enough that if they don't look lower than directly in front of them, they won't see me. I cannot enter my grandmother's salon without an adult present. The holiday tree is in place. I managed to get away with sneaking outside to enjoy the gifts, but what i truly want is something else.

A vintage piano is leaning against the wall. My grandfather's teeth were yellow, much like the keys. The notes have eerie echoes that like the ghost bells of a lost ship. I frequently come in here merely because the piano is calling. The slightest touch of color is enough to draw my attention and cause the air around it to ripple in enormous waves.

The notes sound so depressing when i play them. It's a lonely place. I once questioned him about it in the evening. He answered, "because i'm haunted," and i was instructed to place my ear to his bottom, which is the flat wooden panel that sits in front of your shins when you play. When i pushed my right face against the piano, it said, "now play a few notes," and i heard it. I made contact while raising my left arm so that my face remained in place. I could hear a variety of voices talking over each other beneath the chords above. Since there were so many of them, i was unable to understand what they were saying.

"who are they?" i said after standing up. History, the piano said in response. They are trapped, it stated. If no one plays with me, they can't leave, and i can't breathe with all of them here. I don't care if you play me poorly, he was saying; all i want is to be touched. Because i am a very delicate being and the ghosts are suffering greatly, touch me very softly, very gently, very gently, just barely.

You still haven't informed me where the sounds are coming from, i remarked. He claimed not to want to tell me. He responded, "why?" because of the war, it stated. A child shouldn't be exposed to combat, it stated. People don't converse, so their emotions are directed onto musical things, he claimed. Ghosts are things that people don't want to remember, it declared.

On christmas eve, since baby jesus can't arrive before midnight, we kneel in front of the manger in the living room, set him there, and sing all the songs that make me cry.
I needed my father's assistance to get off my knees and climb the stairs to the bed. The christmas carols were in my body, which made it difficult for me to walk. They twisted and bent me so that i was unable to stand straight. My father is aware of the fact that i cry to music. He doesn't find it strange. I constantly fear that it shows that i'm strange, that the songs make me cry and get paralyzed, and that i'm still a child. He plays "scarlet ribbons" for me as i'm snug in bed. His tone of speaking is depressing. It is terribly depressing. As i am.

   Scarlet ribbons, lovely ribbons
   Hair ribbons in a bright red color.

The tune has me in awe. That the capo di tutti capi can exceed parents, that there are things like angels, that angels leave ribbons, that children's prayers are heard, and that angels can answer questions.
I want tunes that transport me to that other realm, not tapes, though. Reality isn't to my taste. After three minutes, i don't want to be trapped there once more and forced to wait till another opportunity to escape presents itself.

My grandparents

A cabinetmaker, MY FATHER'S FATHER. He erected a wood and wire mesh aviary that spans the bottom of his garden, where he keeps canaries and homing pigeons. I like him a lot. In comparison to my mother's father, he is plump. He also has a giggly, smoky chuckle.

I used to bring him to the aviary so I could see him fly the pigeons carrying messages in tiny barrels attached to his feet, then fly back to him on empty feet. I used to wrap my entire hand around his index finger to do this. I once requested that he text me Hello God from Scamp after he asked me if I would like a text from a fat bird.

My grandfather explained to me that I was given the moniker Scamp because I was the most audacious of all of my mother's sons, and a scamp is a rascal. But after saying that, he flung his head back and laughed wildly. His eyes became so joyful, and he appeared to be a large kid. He admired my boldness. He was possibly the most courageous of his mother's boys.

He takes my grandmother out for a stout alone every night since they are in love. When I knock on their door in the summer, I enjoy to watch them walk down the street. In the Liberties neighborhood of Dublin's city center, which used to be a working-class area and was now home to Guinness and other breweries, they met on the same street, Francis Street. But when my father was twelve years old, his family was forced to leave the Liberties and relocate to Crumlin, a more residential area close to the city's heart. Because of this, Keeper Road, where my mother's parents also reside, is also where my father's parents live. As a result, my parents also met there, just like my father's parents did.

As a bread delivery boy, the father of my mother dresses in a vintage black vest with a pocket watch, a long black coat, and black slacks. He appears to be De Valera on a diet because he is quite tall and thin.

His and my grandmother's home is typical of those of the elderly. Along with Padre Pio, Mary, and Jesus, there are weathered pictures of potatoes all over the wall and above the fireplace. There is a beautiful red Sacred Heart bulb mounted on the wall halfway up the winding stairs. When the other lights are out, nobody wants to climb up there because it's so terrifying.

The father of my mother dislikes ladies who apply cosmetics. He describes them as "Jezebels". He frequently makes biblical insults. When the name of so-and-so is uttered, "Judas!" will be shouted. Also "Jesus crawling!" He only wants silence in life, but because he is from Westmeath, he cannot pronounce silence properly. When we are being too loud, he roars, "Enough! Quite!" at us over his newspaper. We giggle, which prompts him to roar once more.

When it's just him and me at night, I stand behind his chair and softly rock him to sleep as atonement for torturing him. In order to maintain my movements smooth and not waking him up, I create music in my thoughts to match the chair's pace. It repeats one, two, three, one, two, three, one, two, three.

July 1977
DEAD IS ELVIS. I'm crying so hard that I'm unable to make my bed. My body won't function. I keep attempting to fling the sheet onto the bed, but my arms are useless. My legs don't work, so I try to crawl across the bed holding a corner in each hand, but I can't. My mother and I have a falling out because I don't make the

bed. I'm too ashamed to explain why I keep rising up from my knees and leaking tears and snot upon the crisp linens. She might be an Elvis fan as well. He must be aware of my true causes in secret, I suppose. He doesn't seem to mind the bed all that much. He never genuinely becomes angry, which is extremely unusual.

Since Elvis is no longer here, I need a new father. Because my mother doesn't like him, I haven't seen my father in a while, but he isn't dead. They are essentially not supported, in fact. When they are together, it is ominous. To be alone with our father, though, is not particularly threatening. She is unique though.

I already have God, so I'm not looking for another father. And because I communicate with God, he sends me things. He is undoubtedly the best parent. But I'm still a kid. Thank God I lack a voice because I need a father's voice. Why do I appreciate the vocals? I have no idea why. I've been known to desire to hug folks when I hear their voices. But I'm terrified of hugging.

If you try to give me a hug, my body won't cooperate. My Aunt Lily is upset because I like her. I won't embrace her. I genuinely desire. However, I suddenly halt, and in my mind I see a mountain of wolves who are so heavily covered in blood that they are immobile. Only one of the wolves runs, and it is the one that was at the bottom of the pile when the incident occurred. It also lacks blood. You're looking for assistance.

A while has passed since I last saw my grandma, who is the mother of my mum. She has a lovely, gentle voice. She enjoys me. She claims that I am sincere and never apologize if I don't really mean it. She permits me to consume all forbidden foods. When I'm in her bed, she can put me to sleep by simply gazing into my eyes. I enjoy listening to his watch tick. It encourages me to play music. She was the last person I saw when I was around six years old. With my birthday gift, he rode all the buses from Keeper Road. My mom refused to let her in. As I was sitting on the steps, my grandmother sobbed and watched me from outside the door. He exhibited large eyes of fear. He pleaded with my mom. I was on her mind. His tan coat was on him. My mother received the gift from her. Grandma still couldn't get in the door due of the chilly December weather, despite my mother's assurance that she could open it on the stairs and force her to go. Since my birthday falls on a holy day, my grandma enjoys it because she loves God just as much as she loves me.

It was a set of white pajamas covered in tigers. I cherished them. Knowing I couldn't let my face grin at my grandmother, I forced my eyes to do so. She followed suit. But tears were streaming down her face. I haven't seen her since, as I already mentioned. She smokes, and I enjoy the way she smells, so I started smoking properly. I'm a big pray-er, she informed me. She said, "I love God." All I ask is that He stay by my side.

One morning after Elvis, I heard a gentle man singing to a young girl, telling her she didn't need to cry any more. I head over to the turntable. Joe, my brother, must play it once more. I ask, "Who is he?" and he responds, "Bob Dylan." I can tell from the album cover that it is so lovely that it appears as though God took a breath from Lebanon and changed into a man.

When my brother is not home, I am not permitted to play the album. He has a summer job, so I wait every day by the window. I turn the corner as I dash out into the street to hunt for him. I have no idea when he will return home. When he is not around, nothing is secure. Little girls don't appeal to my mother.

The singing of this Dylan man is good. I refer to him as Man from Lebanon in my brain. Across her chest, a baby carrier that is empty is hanging open. I sneak in there. He has a voice that is comforting. He likes girls and is quite kind. I am sleeping on his chest.

So I stopped requesting permission to live with individuals in Glenageary by knocking on their doors. Since I was around six years old, I had been doing that occasionally. In any case, they always take me home because they think my mother is like other people's mothers. Dylan is not easily deceived. However, a few of them handed me cheese balls and other things. When I knocked on the door, a family was holding a Tupperware party. I was crying, so the kind woman allowed me in. She said she could stay for a bit but not stay with me. Because there were many people, I decided to sit underneath the table. She generously handed me food. I'd have preferred to remain with her. My mother was excellent at the door when he first brought me home. In any case, Bob is a lot better father than Elvis. That's what I was thinking the entire time his knee was pressing my belly into the wall.

LOURDES

JUST FIVE DAYS AGO, WE RETURNED FROM LOURDES. A bit over the top. Let's imagine that my mother had a "episode" and that I had to beg and pull a priest to come aid her because it was the only reason we had gone there.

14

The others had to go because the trip was my desired confirmation gift, therefore that's why I went there. Deal being, Mary, mother of Jesus, could look into aiding mine. I kept my thoughts about doing that to myself. They simply assume that since i've been reading about Lourdes for so long, I must be obsessed with the whole thing. My grandmother told me about it in honor of my birthday and because the woman who saw the Virgin Mary there in the nineteenth century shared the same middle name, Bernadette, as me.

No treatment had been found for my mother's lunacy the day I left Lourdes and came back to Dublin, so I made the decision to go and catch priests at four o'clock in the afternoon. I dragged my selected victim by the sleeves in protest since he wasn't as ready to get to work as I was and was instead strolling along the basilica gates with his newspaper. He finally gave in because I was too much for him (I made his eyes wide), and even though that was the only product his employers employed him to market, he looked at me like I was crazy for believing in miracles in Lourdes.

I told him the spooky tale I was about to tell as I pulled him up the street with one hand behind his back and the other on his sleeve to prevent him from running away because I had already told my mother I was going to purchase ice cream. Pitching my mum on how she met me in the hopes that she would do a better job of persuading him than she did with the Lourdes tale.

He then enters his room. I watch the stunning French women in the hotel's little lobby as they make a valiant effort to not appear attractive because they are in Lourdes.

After a while, he descends, holding the newspaper under his arm and gazing fixedly at the ground while donning a black cowboy hat. He nods for me to follow him as he passes my chair. He says, "There's nothing I can do for her," and advises me to pray until I am eighteen and am able to leave home, unless I am able to leave sooner.

Oh, wonderful, I'm thinking. A clergyman without hope. How on earth did it end up parked here?

Look, a few years ago, I experienced my own Lourdes miracle. I was plagued by a wart. On the little toe of the left foot. Large, unpleasant, and with a black center. It was just like the girl who couldn't move her heart in the ancient folk ballad who loves Anachie Gordon.

They therefore hired me to travel to the hospital where the wart would be medically removed, which is really magnificent because it meant that I would be lavishly treated for at least two days, receive a lot of compassion, and require the utmost courtesy from everyone. Not to mention that she would miss a few days of school and that the hospital would likely serve ice cream and jam.

My mother brought me to the restroom the night before I entered and applied some Lourdes holy water on my wart that my grandma had given her years earlier. The wart vanished in the morning. Completely and utterly vanished. There was no sign of him ever being there; nobody would have known. So, unlike my priest friend, I am aware of the reality of the Lourdes miracles.

We had used a travel agency to get to Lourdes. Bus for tourists to pick you up at the airport. Twenty or so more tour participants rode along with us as we drove. We didn't simply stop at Lourdes; we also visited the convent where Saint Bernadette resided and passed away after encounters with Our Lady in the town of Nevers.

Every day, visitors came in to see her tiny body, which was displayed in a Snow White cabinet. It was a repulsive sight. It brought to mind the Dublin Zoo. A crocodile was kept in a glass enclosure that was exactly the same length and width as its body, preventing it from moving, and it was partially submerged in water with its back exposed. There was a chasm with the ceiling at the top of the glass. The older children tried to disturb the crocodile, which was immobile, by throwing coins through the opening so that they would land on its back. What did the zoo staff do with all the coins, I wonder?

In the first 30 years following Bernadette's passing in 1879, her body was exhumed three times so that people might use various portions of her bones for altars. Evidently, if an altar doesn't have some remains of the deceased, it is not hallowed. Sounds more demonic to me than divine.

Our tour guide on the bus was J. He was really kind to me and worked for the neighborhood travel business back home. He told folks what they would see if they looked left or right out the window while sitting up front and spoke into a microphone. However, when they started singing together, my mother repeatedly suggested that I sing "Scarborough Fair," which I dutifully performed with a lot of emotion because I had a love on J. When we all arrived home, I was disappointed because I missed seeing him every day.

He had been singing the song to himself while sighing. I grew bored of doing that today and made the decision to walk the two or more miles to the travel agency to propose to her.

17

When I arrived during noon, J. Was already at his desk conducting a phone call. My heart started to race out of panic. I had never considered the possibility that he might be married. Perhaps he was speaking to her. He ended the call and arrived to find me at the door. He waved me in while expressing surprise that a girl had risen to the level necessary to plan a potential trip through a travel agency.

I explained that I needed a private conversation with him. I was too lovesick to eat, so J. Led me to a tiny kitchen, sat me down at the tiny round table, poured me a glass of milk, and asked if I wanted some cookies.

I submitted a written statement instead of speaking up because I lacked the strength to do so and because I had planned ahead for this possibility. He read it while beaming a smile as the sun lit up his attractive brown beard via the open window. He neatly folded my letter after reading it and asked if he might keep it. Though he was too old to marry me or even be my boyfriend because he was thirty, he claimed it was the most beautiful thing he had ever read. However, he promised that one day he would meet a man my age and would be better.

In addition, he claimed that he was the kind of man that cherished other men. He had to explain a little bit to me because I had never heard of anything such before. He claimed that occasionally, God simply makes men fall in love with other men or women fall in love with other women. He mentioned that people truly weren't in favor of guys liking men, so he asked if I mind if I kept what he said to me. He claimed that people occasionally did not understand what God loved and that they did not always share that love.

18

J. Advised me to never think that any form of love, if it is true love, is wrong and to always have the courage to confess my feelings to someone because it was brave of me to tell him and it made him feel extremely happy. He explained that not all mature men were as certain of their feelings as he was, and that it was inappropriate for an adult to act like a boyfriend to a child. As a result, he advised him not to tell other older men that he loved them after today.

I explained to him that the reason I liked him was because he was good. He therefore advised me to always make sure the people I love are kind. Then he declared that he was going to be my friend and that I could visit him whenever I wanted for milk and cookies.

He wasn't upset as a result because he was so kind to me and I made him smile. I was very pleased of myself for being so brave as I walked home, daydreaming about my future boyfriend. Gary, a man who lives close by, frequently asks me to accompany him to the club. Because she is so severe, I haven't asked my mother, but I might now.

.

MY AUNT FRANCIS

I am six and she is sixteen. Down syndrome affects her. She spends the entire week with the nuns in a nursing facility on Navan Road since my grandmother and grandfather are too old to properly care for her. She does, however, visit every weekend, and I adore her. She adores everyone and everything; she is like a giant walking heart. She is perfect; she has nothing but nice qualities. She exudes elegance and delicacy. She is the only person my mother adores, and she has little hands like her sister, my mother.

When Frances comes home for the weekend, I'm frequently at my grandmother's. Frances brings me upstairs to her room, where she locks us in, and takes the yellow record player that resembles a suitcase that belonged to my grandfather. All of the records in her collection are by the Irish pop artists Danny Doyle and Luke Kelly. Danny Doyle is the love of Frances' life. I'll hear her exclaim, "Isn't that lovely? Isn't that beautiful? In his amusing habit of speaking through his nose. She'll pat me on the head if I don't concur that it's great. But he is not at all endearing. He appears to consume too much beer and sports a beard.

Every time he plays a record, he places the record player on the bed, and I have to hold the lid while he reads out every word that is printed on the cover and labels, front and back, inside and out. She assists me if I am unable to speak by pacing the room like a teacher.

She also has me feel the entire record's packaging with my hands, my face, and even my fingers and palms. It smacks me if I don't move slowly and touch every millimeter.

She enjoys playing with her many baby dolls. She fashions their clothing. My mother assists her since she used to create dresses before she was married, but in Ireland, married women aren't allowed to work any more.

Brenda is the name of Frances' preferred doll. However, Brenda and I unintentionally broke up, and Frances hasn't forgave us. Every time he sees us, he remarks, "You guys broke Brenda." My cousin nibbled the beak off my favorite stuffed animal, a penguin named Charlie that my father got me when I was working somewhere, so I can relate to how you feel. I will never speak to my cousin again since I no longer like him. I'm not quite as polite as Frances.

THE TRAIN

This week, I return to school after a three-month hiatus. Then I repeatedly pretended to be sick at my desk so the nuns would send me home once more. They didn't even have to be Oscar winners for me to get away with only Golden Globe-worthy performances after what occurred because they were so worried about me.

Sweet! It seemed as though I would have been sent home if I had blinked excessively. I'm generally the mean girl since I always take other people's lunches (especially the peanut butter sandwiches), clothes, and cash from the school's instructors' bags for the candy shop. Teaching space.

I frequently accompany Sister Clotilde to the chapel so she can pray for me to stop stealing. It hasn't worked thus far. However, my mum likes it when I steal.

I used to deny having been forced to do it by my mother when teacher Mrs. Sheils questioned me about it. I questioned the origin of the welts on my legs and the one above the once-hugely swollen black eye I had.

"It's your mother, isn't it?" she would say. But I'd contest it.

My mother threatened to murder me if she learned what I told her. Given how beautiful Mrs. Sheils is, I felt horrible for lying to her. He likes me, though I'm not sure why. I want to be his girlfriend. Every afternoon I want to go home with her. Every time she declared she wasn't my mother, it appeared as though she was going to cry. She would become all crimson, reach into her bag, and hand me cash for candy while softly petting my face as my grandmother does.

When I observe the other girls, who have their mothers' arms around them as they stroll down Merrion Avenue after school, I become envious. That's because I'm the young person who cries out in panic on the final day of class before summer vacation. Because I am aware that if I bring my field hockey stick home, my mother will beat me with it all summer long, I have to act as though I lost it. However, he will substitute the carpet sweeper's stick. She will force me to strip off everything, spread my arms and legs out on the floor, and allow her to sweep the sweeping brush over my privates. I have to keep repeating "I'm nothing" or else it will keep stepping on me. He claims he wants to rupture my womb. I had to plead with her for "mercy." I was given the award in kindergarten for being able to roll into the tiniest ball, but my instructor never discovered how I managed it.

I became a follower of Jesus after my mother laid me on the kitchen floor one night and I saw him in my brain. I was covered in cereal and coffee powder and was completely naked. I curled up so my mother could kick my ass as she was yelling all these awful things. Jesus was suddenly in my thoughts, hanging on His crucifixion on a small stone hill.

I never invited him; he just showed up. She was wearing a long white robe, and blood was pouring from her heart through the garment and into the ground before flowing into my heart and streaming down the hill. He declared that His blood would fortify my heart and that He would return to me all the blood that my mother had taken. So I concentrated on Him. I laid on the floor after my mother had finished with me until I noticed that he had locked his bedroom door. After that, I cleaned up everything I had trashed and set the table for breakfast.

When I didn't ask him to, the Holy Spirit once came and sat next to me. It took place as follows:

My sister's clothing, which was now mine, was missing a button. Additionally, we were scheduled to spend the weekend at the home of my mother's friend. Once more, they stripped me, beat me, and my mother removed the lightbulb from my room before locking me up and leaving with the others. I hunt for blank pieces of paper when I'm terrified and write since I can't express my anger toward my mother in words. In order to prevent her from discovering my writing, I first tear the pages into little bits, which I then consume.

It happened on a Friday. I searched my room when it grew dark until I located a pencil and paper. I emailed God. I begged for assistance. Right in front of my bed, he was knelt on the ground. A little, white, very misty cloud then appeared out of nowhere and sat to my left, a bit behind me, where it remained all night.

On the other days, however, the Spirit did not appear.

I went the entire weekend without eating anything and peed on the floor. When my mother returned, she was upset and struck me as a result. Later that day, I had to visit the hospital because I was experiencing excruciating stomach discomfort. The sweet young physician replied, "This child has not eaten." I didn't have the goulash my mum claimed I had.

Before this one, he locked me up and departed once more, but that evening my father arrived, broke down the door, and took me to the doctor. I'm not sure how he discovered my presence. When he noticed all the dried blood on my face, he became upset. In the car, we don't talk much.

Additionally, he repeatedly trapped me under the stairs.

I can hear Mrs. Sheils calling my name in my head when I'm at home.

Sister Clotilde can be heard only addressing me by name. I'm unsure of your opinion of me. It seems to do so somewhat. She just doesn't grin much, and since she's the director, I suppose she shouldn't either. Being a nun must be incredibly dreary. I'm terrified that God will push me toward wanting to be one. Even though I feel called to work for him since he is so wonderful to me, I frequently hope that he won't.

I was ordered to bed for the daytime the last time I heard Clotilde speaking in my brain at home because I had called Princess Anne "pregnant." He was furious at being told to go to bed. Clotilde's voice woke me up the next moment, and as I turned to gaze at my locked bedroom door, the handle dropped all the way, opening the door but leaving no one inside. To find out if my mom had opened the door, I went to the living room. I don't know who answered the door because he claimed he hadn't been upstairs. Maybe Clotilde truly was there.

Soon after, my sister and I were waiting at Blackrock Station for our train to Glenageary after school. A train sped by, and a fourteen-year-old blond lad in a gray school uniform opened a door, brushing up against my right side of the head.

My sister and I boarded our own train as soon as it arrived, got off at our stop, and then walked about a mile up the steep hill to our house even though I was bleeding so badly that my gray school trench coat was soaked from shoulder to knee. My mother was upset that I didn't keep my ticket so I could file a lawsuit against the passengers on the train. I was on the couch when the doctor arrived and stitched my head. My hair was very long. When he was finished, my hair was covered in blood, but for some reason, he advised against washing it for a month. So it became extremely pungent. He also advised me to spend the night in my mother's room, where she would keep an eye on me in case I fainted. I enjoyed myself then with her. He prepared a floor bed for me. She also taught me how to sew during the day while the others were at school and made me banana milkshakes.

I purposefully fainted when I returned to school because of this. Then she would love me and keep me at home.

LOST IN THE MUSIC

In light of what transpired after my brother Joe went away, I requested that my mother's physician admit her to the hospital. He agreed to meet her close to our house after she called the police, who then issued an APB. She drove me along in the automobile. Joe entered and informed her that he would never return home. She threatened to put me in the car's passenger seat and drive into oncoming traffic in order to harm me and push the car back if he didn't, she said. He didn't think she was real. He then exited the vehicle and started his automobile.

She then did. I was the passenger when he purposefully collided with another vehicle. Fortunately, we both felt fine. I yelled at him, though.

I made his doctor a call when we arrived home. He then arrived and offered to take her to the hospital out of concern for us.

I am unable to visit my mum in the hospital with my brothers. I'm relieved because it means I won't have to inform him of my termination from the cafe. They discovered that I had stolen fifty-four pence, but they had been aware of my ongoing theft of cash. I am unable to stop stealing. I lost my job at the clothes retailer because I stole skirts and cardigans for my mother. As well as Easter, we all have summer jobs. Particularly in eateries. We exaggerate our ages.

Since they took her to the hospital, we have spent the majority of the summer alone in the house without any visits from anyone, not even the doctor. We are really savoring every moment.

Ballet dancer is what I want to be. I'm a huge ballet fan. I only make drawings of feet wearing pink or red pointe shoes. I wear pointe shoes when I dance, but I put them on too quickly, which would worry my teacher. Although it's terrible for your feet, I can't quit since I enjoy it so much. I can do anything on my own but I'm too nervous to dance in front of people. I adore my pink, satin-ribbon-adorned shoes more than anything else on the planet. When my sister and I visited the Hospital de la Rotonda to request plaster of Paris so that we could create a mold for the slippers, the doctor informed us that the Rotonda exclusively cared for infants and that no plaster of Paris was available.

I'm a huge fan of Margot Fonteyn. She is so stunning. Colored pencils are used to draw the fire bird. Rudolf Nureyev has my heart. And when they dance together, it appears as though they are a bird and a dove.

One Christmas, my mother gave me a wonderful book about Margot Fonteyn. I use tracing paper to sketch over the photographs in pencil before drawing and coloring them on regular paper.

But until my back is cured, my ballet instructor has said, we can't continue. He claimed that it can be fixed by some people. My entire life, it has been crooked and bowed over. My spine won't straighten. Since the train crash, she claims, it has gotten worse. I received a letter for my mum from her.

When the ballet music starts, the world seems to round me like the whirling dervishes i've seen on television. They're just spinning so quickly that I can't see them. The only thing I can add is that there are planets, space, pinks, greens, bright and dark blues, reds, and sparkles. However, because they are so foggy, they are the sort of colors that you can see through.

As I noted in a young age:

Despite not being a person, there is someone in music.
He reaches out to touch me, but he's not human.
It's constructed of space and is dark blue and green.
He wants to encircle my waist with his arms.
He wants to dance and make me spin with him.
Seems to know who I am, although I'm not sure why.

I also adore Sister Sledge and other disco artists. We always watch Top of the Pops, and I listened to a lot of tunes on the radio in the drive. I adore the line "54-46 was my number." The reggae songs "Israelites" and "Uptown Top Ranking" are also two of my favorites. Except for those three songs, which I adore, i've never listened to any reggae.

The roots of "Uptown Top Ranking" are exact.

I also listened to the Impressions, whose song "Fool for You" is about a man who falls in love with a cruel lady. It's brilliant because they managed to make the music sound like a clown loitering around.

I adore David Bowie as well. As a part of the Marc Bolan show, I attended. Marc Bolan looks like he's pretending to be someone, but David Bowie isn't faking, so I'm not sure what to think of him. He sings the way the teachers encourage everyone to sing and is neither uninteresting nor boxy. It speaks for itself. Marc Bolan has a distinctive voice. He wouldn't need a different voice if he enjoyed his own, which leads me to believe that he dislikes himself.

Bob Marley, a different reggae artist, was on TV. He had really long hair that was parted and was dressed in a blue shirt. I slept in a lot. I had no idea what he was singing about when he sang about stirring something up.

"Stairway to Heaven" and "Freebird" were two songs that my brother Joe played for me on Irish radio station Radio Nova. They're great, and "Freebird" is my favorite. The singer of "Stairway to Heaven" claims that the lady can buy the staircase but you can't, which I find hard to believe.

On the garage roof, Joe and I were jamming out to "Freebird" and a song about huskies peeing in the golden snow. We play the part of a band. When the others are not around, I go up there by myself and jam to "Honky Tonk Women." I shake my long hair over my face in the manner of headbangers.

The Sex Pistols are fantastic. "Anarchy in the UK" is fantastic. And "God Save the Queen" and "Pretty Vacant." Moreover, I adore Stiff Little Fingers and the Boomtown Rats. I adore all the yelling.

In music, anything is possible to say that you cannot in real life. Any loud electric guitar is my favorite. The song "Idiot Wind" by Bob Dylan was played to me by my brother. He speaks venomously to someone while being really enraged. He has great bravery. He doesn't always act like a gentleman.

In the garage, I recently discovered an old, damaged transistor radio. I believe it might have come from my granddad. It may be really old, but I'm not sure. It works after I disassembled it and put it back together. Even now, I have no idea how I did it. At night, I put it under my pillow and calmly listen. The song about the light shining through a cloudy day, the song about a clown crying, and the song "Just My Imagination" are all songs

I enjoy. In addition, I enjoy Ray Charles and the Supremes. Moreover, Dire Straits and Elvis Costello.

Ireland's main radio station, RTÉ, regularly features my mother. It's so dull and miserable. Never do they converse or play music that is uplifting. They are all quite depressing songs, such as "Tears on the Phone" and the one about the art teacher who instructs a young student that flowers must always be red. Also playing are show bands. The show bands are the worst. They dance to incredibly ridiculous tunes like The Shadows while wearing awful glittering clothes and playing dreadful renditions of country and western songs. They are Irish.

You speak all day, especially on RTÉ. Dull, dumb, depressing, or square things. There was a lot of press coverage on the fighting in the north as well. When I hear about bombs, fire, elderly people suffering, people crying, tanks, soldiers, people hurling things, and even small toddlers watching in the streets, I get quite afraid.

And that disgusting Ian Paisley character screaming with his eyes wide open while wearing a priest's robe. My mother claims that the devil always appears as a priest, thus I'm positive that it is the devil. When I watch it on TV, I am immobile. When he enters the room without my father, it bothers me. When I was younger, I had to find my father because he was out seeing Laurel and Hardy. Laurel then fell down the bathroom sink drain, which made me very angry. I'd rather it had been the chap from Paisley.

We are all expected to stand up when the national anthem is played on RTÉ television each night just before it goes off the air.

A woman named Frankie hosts a terribly depressing radio program where she reads letters from women with awful partners in a deep, raspy voice. Bad boyfriends are those who don't propose to their girls or who seek sex with them prior to becoming engaged. Additionally, he receives messages from guys who are too nervous to propose to their women. And letters containing accounts of heartbreak, devastating loss, and broken hearts.

Additionally, the station frequently plays Marianne Faithfull's unhappy song, in which she laments, "Someday i'll get over you." My poor mother paid for the album. I'll go insane if I hear it once more. She might move on from my father, but i'll never get over listening to that awful music.

The same is true of Marianne's rendition of "The Ballad of Lucy Jordan," a song by Shel Silverstein about a lady who goes insane.

I now have a new position. In a club A disco is a place where people go to dance to disco music rather than the uninteresting Irish dance music that small squares listen to, my mother's lover told me, therefore I believe him. I put a lot of heavy foundation, blush, mascara, and lipstick on even though I'm just thirteen. When I went in and told the manager my age, he accepted me!

This is the best work i've ever done thus far. I mean, I dress nicely in black with a white blouse. I took them both from Dunnes, a major chain of department stores.

I'm responsible for distributing the pink dinner tickets. Men must place a dinner order before they may start drinking when they enter. So they line up for lunch first, then to get a numbered ticket from me. The best curry you can eat is generally terrible, nothing like the curry my mum makes. I enjoy it even though it causes intense afterburn on my face. Since onions don't make me cry, I always chop them when she makes them.

The males are friendly, and I enjoy how the atmosphere becomes hazy and slightly inebriated. I enjoy the disco lights and the way they reflect off of the enormous disco ball that is suspended from the ceiling in the center of the dance floor. I enjoy how it is difficult to see anyone clearly due to the smoke and pillars on the dance floor.

Because the DJ said he could, I arrive at work an hour and a half before the business starts. He regularly arrives earlier than me. He needs to practice his set, so as he performs at maximum volume, he switches on the disco lights and the smoke machine for me. I then put on my ballet flats and my shiny blue stretchy disco pants, which are so tight that my mother would kill me for wearing them. I took them as well.

I make the DJ swear not to look while I have the floor to myself for a solid thirty minutes. He treats me well. He does not glance. I am aware because I continue to watch him. He settles down behind his mixing console and works on his to-do lists.

STILL LOVE ME TOMORROW?

Okay, i made a mistake. But it's not a sin because i didn't realize it was wrong. At least, the bible states that. Now that i am aware that it is wrong, if i were to repeat it, it would be wrong. I'm excellent as long as i don't repeat the mistake.

I was demonstrating a humorous pointing technique my father taught me years ago to my friend while we sat in pizzaland. The waiter mistook her for summoning him. Not me. But it soon became apparent that he believed i was making out with him. He then began to make out with me. This was pretty flattering because he was attractive and american. Cool accent and bleach blonde semi-dreadlock hair. He inquired my age, and even though i'm only 14, i replied, "eighteen." he believed me since i was heavily made up.

American males are great and never disagreeable. All irish males are complete jerks. They lack any sexual appeal. Despite our mother's warnings, my sister and i used to strike up conversations with every mormon male in town simply because they were americans. In their suits, they appeared so dashing and like movie stars. They labored in couples while attempting to convert irish people on the streets (they were so charming they believed it may work). But all they were doing was changing what young women wanted from young men to older men, especially older guys in suits.

My sister and i invited two of the mormons over to chat about the bible in their home. Because i enjoy discussing the bible, it was just a falsehood. They made us popcorn and explained the differences between being a mormon and a catholic while sitting there in their white shirts and jackets off. There was nothing they actually stated that i can recall. I used to imagine myself ecstatically contentedly married to one of them, living on a farm, and having nothing better to do at the end of the day than to discuss the scriptures and go naked and slide on him in his suit.

    Anyway, this poor waiter, paul, thought i was eighteen and started flirting with me. He offered me to go with him to his apartment in smithfield, but i had never had sex, so i had no idea that what he had in mind was sex. Truly. I believed that while we wouldn't have sex, we would at least make out like people my age do.

    However, after a time of kissing, it was clear that "the whole enchilada" was needed. I reasoned that i would eventually have to lose my virginity. The majority of my pals have. Because i hadn't, and this was my big break, it wasn't good at all. I crawled into bed with him, thrilled that my deflorist was an american, but yet quite anxious. I was anxious because i was unsure of your intended actions. I had only ever taken one sex education class. One afternoon, a chubby old nun suddenly burst into our classroom; we had never seen it before and had no idea why it was there. Without saying a word, he grabbed up the chalk and quickly sketched a huge, erect penis pointing upwards. It had a massive set of balls underneath and must have stood approximately a foot tall.

    We were giggling on the floor before i had done drawing. Literally holding on to avoid going potty. She was already lost when she turned back to begin the speech she had planned; he had lost control of the space. We were unable to stand. He never considered getting rid of the penis. Instead, she repeatedly pleaded for order as she stood in front of him. He finally fled the space. The end of sex education came then.

I've read the book the joy of sex by my stepmother. The drawings of the man and woman are in black pencil, which makes it kind of horrific. Both of them are quite unattractive. He's got a hideous beard. I hadn't read the book at all since they turned me off to the thought of having sex. I've gained no new knowledge.

In the book, there is a drawing that really freaked me out. It is in a chapter about skills that women must possess. It serves as a warning that if you don't complete them precisely, you risk being dumped. The woman grabs her clothing to get dressed and depart while the male lies in bed yelling and pointing at the door. Come outside and never again leave my bedroom door dark, he is requesting.

I'm lying in bed with paul, an american, and i'm wondering, "oh god, what do i do?" however, i didn't have much time to worry. He first struggled to enter inside of me, and as soon as he succeeded, he realized he had never had sex before. I gradually started bleeding.

He afterwards came to the realization that he was not eighteen. He nearly suffered a heart attack when i revealed that i was fourteen. He made me get dressed right away, helped me get a bus home in the pitch-black, and begged me never to lie about my age again because he said it was against the law to have sex with anyone under the age of eighteen and he might get into trouble. Issues involving the police.

I questioned whether i would appear different on the bus. Would the other passengers think to themselves that i'm cool because i'm a female who isn't a virgin anymore?

MY MOTHER'S RECORD COLLECTION

Aside from baking, my mother's other great loves are cooking and music. He attended the city's Cordon Bleu culinary institute. She crafts exquisitely decorated cakes that are wonderful. To purchase dolls for those above, he brings us to the home of a strange old woman. The lady is so elderly, in my opinion, that she should be dead, yet the sugar in her body keeps her alive. His home is cluttered with rugs and dirty.

When the delectable cakes are on display for Easter or Christmas, we only utilize the enormous dining table in the living room. My mother's record collection, however, is dispersed over the remainder of the year like a deck of cards.

Waylon Jennings, Porgy and Bess by Ella Fitzgerald and Louis Armstrong, Bridge Over Troubled Water by Simon and Garfunkel, Johnny Cash's prison recordings, and Simon and Garfunkel's Sounds of Silence are all included. There are numerous Beatles songs, Woodstock, Van Morrison's Moondance, the Velvet Underground, Lou Reed, and the Jungle Book soundtrack. Additionally, dad owns a ton of Elvis recordings; the first album I purchased was an Elvis double album titled Le Roi du Rock 'n' Roll. (I adore Elvis movies, too.

I don't like Frank Sinatra, despite the fact that my mother has a lot of his music. Along with Otis Redding, she also has a boy named Donovan. Jimmy Durante, an older man with a large nose, is the next character. Sing a humorous song about the missing chord; I really like that tune.

It includes music by Dusty Springfield, Nick Drake, Joni Mitchell, Cat Stevens, Stevie Wonder, Mike Oldfield, and a strange Rick Wakeman album titled The Six Wives of Henry VIII. Additionally, he has numerous recordings by renowned Irish operatic tenor John mccormack. She claims that listening to him sing makes her feel as though she has passed on and is now in heaven. Every time he speaks, I feel as though I'm in hell.

Barbra Streisand is my favorite singer from her whole discography. I enjoy seeing your flicks. I adore Funny Girl and Hello, Dolly. She has gorgeous long nails and stylish eyeliner, and she is quite attractive. Both his singing and speaking voices are gorgeous. She doesn't sing like anyone i've ever heard; instead, her voice is much more free-flowing, similar to David Bowie but plainly distinct. Both of them have a raucous bird sound. Everyone else seems submissive. One day, I hope to sing in musicals and compare myself to Barbra. Although I bite them till they bleed, I would also like to see my nails grow. My mother's fingernails are unusually long. She keeps stuffing those foul-tasting items inside mine so I won't bite into them, but they still find their way into my sandwiches.

I adore John Lennon as well. He makes me feel like my brother. I can recall it singing in my living room ever since. His voice has an angelic quality to it. He shares my sense of boldness. And like me, he is furious. I enjoy his irate voice. He is daring to admit that he feels depressed as well. I enjoyed it when he remained in bed. I really wish I could. I like your wife since I adore kitties and think she is adorable. She must have wanted to stay in bed all day since she loves him so much and wanted to embrace him. I want to give you both a big embrace. Do you think they would prefer a girl?

HOW COME I SING

I feel like throwing up, and THE SERGEANT CAN see it. But he won't let me leave. I want to sprint down the road to the old hog farmer Harvey Proctor. I approach him occasionally because he lets me pet the infants. I can't recall how we first connected. He treats me kindly. Both the enormous, fat fathers and the mother sows have strong odors since they spend their entire days lying in foul manure. My dream is to be a pig. I adore infants and their sweet squeaks. Harvey says I can't because it would get too big to leave the house, despite the fact that I really want to bring one home.

I was caught after using a blue laundry marker to draw a large toothy cross-eyed face on the bathroom door of a Dalkey bar last week. After returning a few days later with my collection tin, the bar owner began badgering me. He claimed that he had reported me to the police because he was aware that I was stealing from the collection cans. I quickly made my way to the restroom, where I squeezed out a little window. Since then, I had been living in fear at home, so I made the decision to go visit the sergeant and explain the situation since, if my mother learned that I had been apprehended by the police, I would require police protection.

Even my mum has a theft addiction. As far back as I can remember, it has been. Take money out of the collection basket when it is passed at mass rather than placing money in it. She drove into the night carrying trowels and black rubbish bags to steal the freshly planted young shrubs when the new roundabout on Avondale Road was finished. She returned downstairs and removed the old shrubs when they had been replaced. What he did with them is unknown to me. He took the cross off the wall when he was in the hospital. I was even sent home wearing my school trench coat over his hospital room scale. She visits homes that are up for sale solely to steal items. On the floor surrounding her bedroom, she has a massive stack of books that is about three feet high. Every single one was taken by her. Everything is stolen by her.

I have a theft addiction as well. This is why I enjoy singing hymns. Being such a terrible person is intolerable. For me to be able to live with myself, I must perform a holy act.

I go door-to-door, offering to sell people my stolen flowers from their gardens in exchange for their own flowers. I spent weeks stealing large sums of money from the yacht club's changing facilities, but I was caught when I asked a milkman in a van for money for my quarters and he became suspicious. When the clerk brought me in to try on some ballet shoes, I took a wallet from a bag in the staff area of the shoe store. When I returned to try to repeat it, they detained me and summoned the police, who were, thankfully, extremely polite to me. I pleaded with him not to tell my mother, but he refused.

I began taking first aid classes about a year ago. The course administrators announced that they will be collecting items for Flag Day. You go to people's homes with a can and badges to ask for money, which is then put toward doing good deeds. The prize, they explained, would be a silver Cross pen, and it would go to whoever raised the most money the following Sunday. Because I associate my father with nice pens, I really wanted to win. I traveled from Blackrock to Glenageary to get home, knocking on doors along the way, and when I got there, my tin was practically full. I couldn't wait to tell my mother that I had done something well and had a chance to win the pen.

We have a rough-looking red sofa with a worn-gold pattern. My mother took out the cushions, retrieved a knife from the kitchen drawer, and removed the can's lid. Underneath was heavy-duty metal foil. He cut the aluminum foil by circling the edge with the knife. He then gave me the can back and instructed me to throw the cash on the couch. The coins are stacked in denominations of fifty, ten, five, two, one, and a halfpenny. I should keep the copper coins, she remarked, taking all the silver ones.

I was appalled. However, I continued because she was content with me. He was grateful for the money. I realized that things would be secure if I continued to make money.

Charities set up trailers outside the large city bank and encourage people to donate money on their behalf. When asked who you are, you make up any old name and address after receiving a can and a roll of badges. Not even a check is made. My mother and I have been receiving cans in all shapes and sizes from several charities. None of them have been left untouched. Everyone can trust us because of our fashionable accents. Since the day I returned home with the first aid kit, we have been working on it. We have been spending the night outside of Dublin's bars in order to raise money. On the weekends, we spend hundreds of pounds; occasionally, we have to empty a can in the car before moving on to the next location. It is roughly half on weeknights.

Mom is performing for Sgt. On this chair, almost deserving of an Oscar. Pretending to know nothing about cans and being furious. I want to puke because of this, but the sergeant won't allow me. She wants me to witness her selling me short. She is unaware of his pledge to not imprison me because I gave him the truth. She doesn't mind if they imprison me. The sergeant appears to want to strike him.

I don't believe I still adore her.

A large home filled with priests is located just across the street from my school. One morning, instead of going to class, I rapped on the door. I requested an older woman to open the door for me, and I said that I needed to see a priest alone. He brought me into a sizable, bright living room with a tiny table made of dark wood that had waves in it. She disappeared and came back carrying a tea tray with plates of Madeira cake and flower-patterned china cups and saucers. He advised me to be polite and eat because the priest would arrive shortly. While I waited, the confirmation choir songs began to sing in my head, which got me thinking about them. Except for one, I don't even like them. He suggests that even if you are something awful, God could be able to transform you into something good.

He had brown hair and was a kind and friendly clergyman. He wasn't very elderly, and his voice was soothing. We exchanged words for ages. I informed him that God could perceive me as a thief and that I was. And that, as it is, I am a terrible person. He heard what I had to say to the sergeant today. And I explained to him how I had tried to walk on the carpet while they were on fire by sticking my wooden stilts into the fire in my home.

He listened intently before asking me what I thought I would like to do when I grew up. I admitted to him that I enjoy singing.

He uttered, "Ouch! Did you realize that a singer makes two prayers?

I confessed to him, saying, "I didn't know that, father, but I think it should work for the girls too because I can sing my mother to sleep with 'Don't cry for me Argentina.'"

And don't you recall that a thief who died next to Christ was given paradise as a reward for his repentance? He enquired about my favorite female singers. I confessed to him my love for Randy Crawford. He had me swear that if I find employment, i'll reimburse him for all the money I took. He claimed that in doing so, he'll be at peace with God. He suggested that if I didn't want to wait, I could perform on the street, but I can't play the guitar. To make me seem cool, I only carry my brother's guitar case around Blackrock when it is empty.

But i'll honor my word.

THE HOUSE OF THE RISING SUN, PART ONE

I'm observing my eyes as they reflect in the back seat window of my father's car. I imagine that during my entire life, I will only ever be observed by the same two eyes. I insisted that he make a stop at the record shop so that I could purchase a copy of Bob Dylan's Desire. I moved out of my mother's house months ago, not long after we were caught with the donation cans. Since then, i've been living at my father's house.

His home is a bit disorganized. My father's family, my stepmother's family, and the one they created together are like three separate families. Three of my stepmother's daughters exist. My little brother should be here, but he is still at my mother's place. The oldest is the same age as my sister, the next one is the same age as me, and the following one is the same age as my little brother. So, the son of my father and stepmother is almost five years old. Only my sister, my five-year-old half-brother, my younger stepsister, and my stepmother are well-mannered. My father and I are the only ones left who are entirely incapacitated.

My stepmother Viola, I like her. She is emaciated. She has a soft voice, a soft accent, and a big, toothy smile. She is from Northern Ireland. She speaks French really well and has short blonde hair. He enjoys calligraphy and gives me some tips. She occasionally drinks a glass of sherry and needs assistance getting into bed. She seems so helpless. He reveres the surface that my father walks on. I sincerely hope my mother is there. I get upset with her sometimes because she isn't. I was enraged with her for delaying getting to know my father.

We can't love my stepmother, according to my mother. When we were driving around town, he would point to the shops where he said my stepmother bought clothes and declare, "Only the prostitutes go there." The same thing would apply when I pointed to hotels and nightclubs. My sister and I laughed while also wanting to visit all of those destinations. She told me, "Only prostitutes get their ears pierced," so a few days after I split up with her, I had my ears pierced. Additionally, I significantly shortened my hair because "only prostitutes" do it.

Like me, Viola loves God. We discuss God a lot. She is quite kind and deeply in love with my father. I'm unsure of how she manages. It kind of pulls the trigger. Maybe the reason it works is that he is so gentle. Even if he wanted to lose his temper, he couldn't. We make fun of her when she gets upset with me and my stepsister.

When I was approximately nine years old, my brothers and I spent around nine months living in my father's home. As I previously indicated, I used to steal candy and other items from stores. I was also a pain in the ass, constantly arguing that I didn't have to do anything that Viola ordered me to do. Poor woman, I'm on top of her with my large tongue.

She would take my hand and slap my fingers so gently that I was unable to feel anything, believing that I was behaving really irate. Don't dictate to me because I won't have it, he said in his thick Northern Irish accent with each smack, gritting his teeth as hard as he could but failing to do so. Because she was devoid of evil.

My mother lost custody of my brothers and I when my father left her because she had forced us to live in a hut he had constructed for us in the garden on the day he had gone. We broke down in tears after he left. He suggested we could move into the shack and live there if we truly loved him. When it got dark, I screamed out from where I was kneeling in front of the gable wall to the landing window, pleading with him to let us inside the house. The light in her room turned off, and everything went dark when she remained silent. I had officially lost my mind at that point, and I was also terrified of the vastness of the sky.

I have no memory of what happened after that; nothing until I was holding the judge's hand and walking through the judge's garden because I didn't want to say anything harsh that may cause him additional anguish.

I didn't want to abandon my mother when she realized she had lost us. When our father departed with us, she put on quite a show of emotion, and she continued to cry every time we ran into her on the occasional Saturday. I felt terrible for her. I spent the entire day at my father's house howling exactly like a wolf under my brother John's bed until we were ordered back. Because Freddie Mercury is singing "Bohemian Rhapsody" to his mother, I too spent a lot of time loudly singing along with the music.

My father isn't a cheerful man. I can't say that I'm mad at him. When she sings in the morning bathroom, her voice is sombre and sounds like an opera singer. Long after lunch, he turns blue and goes to bed. I am seated at the table next to her and can sense the sadness seeping up into her eyes from within her womb. He dislikes having me witness it.

It reminds me of someone who has been burned and is frantically searching for fresh water to stand in. He cannot remain motionless. He is dependent on his job. Because he is a guy, he can get away with having my stepmother take care of us savages. I won't hold him responsible for that. If I were him, I would also try to get away with it.

He makes me feel incredibly uneasy. I unintentionally shake my foot pretty quickly as I cross my legs and lean forward on the edge of my seat. Both he and I are not people we actually know. It's not my fault or his; it's my mother's; she kept him from seeing us for such a long time. But she didn't say she wouldn't leave him, so I assumed he simply hadn't shown up, and I carried a lot of resentment at him inside me the entire time. If he instructs me, I get upset and say foul things like, "He has no right to be a parent now." I am a bad guy. I have a problem. He thinks I'm nuts.

I exit through the other door when the poor guy drops me off at school. I'm in love with B, but he doesn't want a girlfriend, so I'm going out with Jerome Kearns while waiting for the Oatlands boys to come over for lunch. I could care less about school. What's the purpose? Getting hugs is the most crucial thing to do, and Jerome is incredibly kind to me. We only exchange hugs and discussions about Pink Floyd and Bob Dylan. He gives me cute names and his shoulders are at the correct height for my head.

When I am aware that our English class will be writing about Yeats poems, I attend. Yeats' writings are like music to me, but they also open up a new sky—the one inside of me. That sky doesn't scare me since it has boundaries. The garden seems to have been carried inside by the poetry, which seem to have all the windows open. The hues of the outside have vanished and I can now see internal scenes. There isn't a terrible cosmos spinning outside of me; instead, what's inside of me is an old, tarnished living room with a massive fireplace made of gray marble. Yeats is insane as he chronicles the tragic Irish republican revolt against the British in "Easter, 1916." What I put in my test in response to the question "No one is laughing now" Was the poet saying anything?

I've been inspired to write songs by Yeats, but I'm not yet ready. He, the old fool, has been in love more often than I have. Always asking a woman to marry him, not understanding why she says no, and finally asking the mother's daughter, which explains why the mother has repeatedly said no. He is a strangeo. It resembles a walrus somewhat. It is quite repulsive. But his poetry are works of art. Although I tire of folks who rhyme desire with fire or pyre, "No Second Troy" is my fave. There must be another choice.

In fact, during the past nine months, i've had three schools expel me. I continue to get caught shoplifting, too. I'm snatching anything that isn't fastened down. I'm not even sure why. My stepmother contacted Irene, a social worker, because things had gotten so horrible. I abhor her. For my pal to wear to the Pretenders performance, I stole a pair of gold shoes, but I got caught. Because I'm the second-fastest sprinter in the class, I stole clothes for my pals. I simply put my things on in the stores, then I quickly leave. I am currently driving my father's automobile and staring out the windshield with my two eyes because Irene told my father and stepmother to send me to this location. I am aware that they are the same eyes I shall always look into.

"the Dawn" is the name of the location, An Grianán.

THE HOUSE OF THE RISING SUN, PART TWO

Jesus in his red and white garments is depicted in a large, full-color statue as you enter High Park and head towards An Grianan. He welcomes you with wide arms. I feel bad for him because he must be shivering. And I ponder why, although being from Bethlehem, she always has a Kerry accent. His eyes and skin should undoubtedly be darker.

There are numerous nuns that reside in this gloomy area. We are not permitted to speak to the several elderly women who are moving around in slippers with their chins resting on their chests. They reside in a different section of the structure.

It is a huge L-shaped structure. A sizable church and a little garden are present. When a nun was being buried, I crept inside to see what she looked like. Her fingernails had dark purple crescents.

The girls keep claiming that the White Lady's spirit roams the garden; they claim she crosses the narrow bridge to the church, but i've never seen her. Additionally, they claim that there are numerous overgrown graves with the name MAGDALENA written on each one. But how is it possible that there are so many people with the same name in one location?

I wonder if the elderly nuns are aware.

Two songs can be played on the record player during your break according to the music policy here, but you must inform the staff in the morning if you want to do so in order to reserve your space. In this manner, everybody gets a chance. The girls were playing Elkie Brooks' "Don't Cry Out Loud" repeatedly in the living room when I arrived in the morning. I had to crouch and hone in on a corner.

Three of the hardwood walls in my cubicle are light blue in color. It has a little bed, a tiny chair, and a tiny dresser. A cloud of orange flowers blows on the other side of what ought to be the fourth wall. I notice a small blue and white statue of the Virgin Mary that has been left in the lattice above the rails when I'm in bed.

The girl in the cubicle next to mine used to peek over the wall separating us when I first started working here and smile like a nosy pixie against the sky. He was quite curious about me. He grilled me with questions at the rate of a machine pistol. I struggled to discover items quickly enough. She enjoys me. She is quite feminine. She is 17 years old. She used to routinely trim her nails and had small, delicate hands. Her manicure was flawless. Her black hair is fairly short, and she has dark skin and large, brown eyes. She resembles Audrey Hepburn, but brunette instead of blonde. She used to regularly pluck her eyebrows and dab on some lip gloss. She once spoke in a ladylike manner. He would respond with, "I know!" if you told him she was lovely that day.

All of the girls, in my opinion, are present because their families do not want them. You repeatedly play "The Logical Song" by Supertramp. She wouldn't be here or anywhere else listening to such a depressing music if I were her mother or father. One needs surgery for a twisted hip. He's already had a few, but before he can have the next big one, he needs to grow a little bigger. Why he isn't waiting with his family is a mystery to me. She is a traveler and only twelve years old.

Your cousin is also present. She's extremely adorable. She likes to travel. She has gorgeous black hair and a deep yellow complexion. He's probably seventeen years old. She is the most stunning woman that God has ever created. They both have such lovely accents and rich voices, and I adore the way they speak.

They speak differently from how most people do. I mimic their speech at my office because I enjoy listening to it. Right as I do it, it sounds like singing.

Twenty-two years old is one of the girls. Supposedly, it has resided here since it was fourteen years old, when I was. I don't want to be here when I'm twenty-two; it makes me nervous. She doesn't appear to be entirely "present." She walks in slippers like those elderly people and has the same expression in her eyes.

She engages in some brief self-talk, as do elderly women. He also licks his lips excessively. Nobody ever pays her a visit. In actuality, family visitors are really uncommon. The girl whose parents are visiting goes down to the small side sitting room by the entrance door where there is tea and everything is extremely formal. The girl's parents occasionally take her out, but they always bring her home. Always, I pray that they won't. I wish they would leave this depressing area behind and run with their son, but they don't.

Even though a slim girl is really scary since she will tell you to fuck off and appear like a wolf when she says it, fangs and all, I like her despite how angry she is. He frequently makes cruel jokes about me. Even if I don't like that, there are aspects of her that I respect. I wish I had the guts to be as obnoxious as her. He expresses all the negative thoughts he has. I only blow mine up when I'm extremely angry and hurt.

She is starting a job in an office. They took us to shop for what appeared to be work attire. I said something that mistakenly made her feel more than just angry and I felt terrible for her when she turned her face away to lean against the door of the ancient Gresham Hotel as we took a break from shopping. She didn't appear violent for a very long time after that. She is a canary in a tiger suit; she is in no way violent.

In the afternoons, they teach us to type upstairs, but in the mornings, John is the one teaching us arithmetic, English, and other subjects. I like him a lot. Because of his kindness and the way he speaks, I truly have a big crush on him. But whether we're studying poetry or short tales, I still don't pay attention. I'm confident that he was thinking, "Hmm, maybe that annoying girl isn't totally useless after all," in his head. For him, it feels like an instantaneous epiphany. As soon as the math book was published, it vanished, and I demonstrate that it is impossible.

On Friday nights, individuals occasionally come to sing with us, including priests in formation. God gives "good people" points for hanging out with the wicked youngsters. Another John, one of the student priests, captured my heart. (I have a thing for folks named John.) Like Master John, this John is a kind person. (As I mentioned, I'm easily seduced.) I thought this John was wonderful because he loves God as much as I do and enjoys talking just about him and songs. I begged him to give up his plans to become a priest and marry me instead, but he declined.

I will never get married at this pace. They continue to reject me.

One evening, the Fureys performed in our tiny concert hall downstairs. The girls were let to go. My favorite song, "Sweet Sixteen," which I always associate with my first love, B, was played. When I came here, I had to leave him and all my other pals behind. The lead singer, Finbar Furey, is reported to have written an instrumental piece when he was twelve years old, which was performed afterwards. It was played with a sort of high Irish whistle. The title of it was "The Lone Boatman." The most gorgeous, melancholy melody i've ever heard. Such suffering from a young person. I felt as though I had a heart of my own. Additionally, nobody here had ever known my heart.

When the audience exited and the band began to pack up, you could find me waiting in the back. I went up to Finbar and told him that listening to his music inspired me to desire to pursue a career in music.

Even though we are now buddies (at the ripe old age of 53), he claims that he cannot recall ever having met me. However, I will never forget the time I spent talking to him. And to this day, I still cry whenever I read his name on a dressing room door, which happens occasionally when we are both performing at the same festivals. Simply because his songs and his music have such a wonderful beauty to them.

When you turn eighteen, they will begin getting you ready for the workforce. They have been training us how to type in order to prepare us for employment in typing groups or offices. In order to acclimate you to the working world, they start allowing you to go out in public on a more regular basis. You had a peculiar day at the office or in the typing pool where you go to work where you go to work. When the girl who looks like a darker version of Audrey Hepburn in the cube next to me started going through this procedure, she ended up meeting a guy from Glenageary, which is the same place I'm from. She fell in love with this guy, and as a result, she became pregnant.

She felt a great deal of joy about it. And filled with enthusiasm and pride. It should come as no surprise that she got in problems with the nuns. The newborn was a boy, and his complexion was so pale that it looked blue, and his hair was as dark as the night. She spoiled him and took care of him, including all of his clothing, in the same manner that she had previously taken care of herself. They were deeply in love.

I really like giving him hugs. I adored the sounds that they made. I couldn't get enough of her scent on her itty-bitty head. He appeared to be baby Moses, for he was wrapped up in his blue and white blanket and was getting his reed basket ready to float down the Nile.

I have no idea whether or not she was aware that they weren't going to let her retain it. I'm not sure if any of us knew about it. However, I don't believe that we did. When they pulled him from their arms and I realized he was gone, I was so stunned that the event has completely escaped my memory. Someone told me that in Ireland, if you are under the age of eighteen and you are not married, you are unable to keep your baby.

Even though her body is still here, she has also passed on now.

Her nails are not filed or shaped in any way. She does not use cosmetics of any kind. You used to have great style, but now it's all gone. He never grins and is never heard talking. She spends the entire day doing nothing but sobbing her eyes out, poor thing. She claims that her parents did not give it to her father, but she is unsure who they did give it to instead. They simply took it with them and then left. Moses had it so hard by himself.

THE HOUSE OF THE RISING SUN, PART THREE

MAYBE FOUR HOSPITAL BEDS WERE LINED UP AGAINST EACH WALL, AND CURTAINS WERE DRAPED AROUND THEM. In the manner of a real hospital. Everything, even the linoleum, the draperies, and the walls, was dyed to look like buttermilk. The lights were dim and a dark yellow tint; they appeared to glow behind the walls, and as a result, light could be seen penetrating through the backs of the cubicles. Because there was nobody working at the time, I had to wait for someone to arrive and inform me where I should sleep. Since there was nobody working, I had to wait. I overheard someone wailing from one of the beds, and another person was yelling "Nurse, nurse." After waiting for fifteen minutes without anyone coming, I decided to take a brief peek into each cubicle. There was an elderly lady dozing in each of the beds. Because I had gone to hospitals in the past and had witnessed some people in their final stages of life, I was able to determine that it was a small hospice. And I realized that these were some of the elderly ladies I had occasionally seen stumbling through the gardens, the people to whom we were strictly forbidden from interacting in any way.

The most recent of numerous successful elopements culminated in many street performances and participation in talent events in Dublin hotels, where I always won five pounds if I took it. Sister Margaret had put me here to sleep as a punishment for the most recent of these elopements, which was the most recent of several successful elopements. In the direction of sung "Don't cry for me Argentina." When I tried to run away the previous time, I made a significant error: I brought another girl with me. An elder young lady. As a result, he ended up fucking a person against the wall of a block of flats, and his companions fled with all of our belongings; consequently, I became terrified and returned to Grianán. After what seemed like two weeks had passed, the girl did not come back. I never saw any of my belongings again, but luckily I didn't lose my new guitar because I didn't set it down once during the entire ordeal.

As they make their way around the outside of the structure, the elderly women don't lift their feet very much, giving the impression that they are a line of ducks following an absent mother. Because there is constantly a nun in their rearview mirror, everything appears to be unusually backwards. The sound that is made by the ladies' slippers is a soft shh-shh. When I see them, I get this very odd feeling, and I'm frightened because there's a courtyard between us that I can't cross to ask them. The way that they all hold their chins to their chests and have their hands folded over their wombs gives the impression that they have committed a terrible crime and are pleading for pardon, or that they are a row of slaves with eerie, quiet shackles on their hands. While I was on my way to the auction.

That night, I slept in the only empty bed I could locate, which was the only bed I could find. The terrified shrieks of the woman who was sleeping next to me continued all through the night. There were additional ladies who called occasionally, but no one came. I tossed over, half sleepy and half awake, trying to figure out why Sister Margaret had gone to such lengths; the typical punishment for breaking the rules was to be sent to Coventry and forced to sleep on your mattress on the floor outside of your chamber and eat by yourself. You are not going to look presentable again until all of the females finish their laundry in time for the meeting on Wednesday evening.

The atmosphere in the laundry area seems a little strange. To begin, there is no sign of a washing machine anywhere in the vicinity. There are a great deal of pipes, around thirty significant white sinks, and a great deal of chandeliers. Everything is built of concrete, and the floor has deep grooves because of the millions of footsteps that have been taken on it. It resembles the rock of Lourdes, which has been worn away over the course of one hundred and thirty years by the hands of people who have rubbed it in the hope of having miraculous children.

At some point, I dozed off, and when I awoke, I had a dream that the elderly woman who worked in the cube next to mine was sitting on my bed, singing "I don't know how to love him" while she shaped her nails. She had a lighter disposition and appeared to be several years younger. After that, the partition walls and curtains were removed, and the elderly women's beds were transformed into rows of graves marked with the word MAGDALENA.

After spending the night at the hospice, I vowed to myself that I would never run away again. When I woke up in the morning, I had a clear understanding of what

Sister Margaret had been attempting to convey to me. The fact that he was aware that she wasn't trying to be malicious was the worst part. I had never seen anything like the nun act that she was putting on. She had intentionally avoided telling me the reason why she needed to go to a part of the building that I was unaware even existed, climb a flight of stairs that I would never have been allowed to climb even if I had asked, knock on a door that she had not been permitted to touch in the past, and enter such a scene when there was no staff present.

She gave me the opportunity to learn the truth on my own: if I didn't stop jogging, I would eventually become one of those elderly women.

A few months after I moved to Grianán, I became aware of the fact that one of the older girls was permitted to attend school since she was working on completing her high school diploma. In other words, she was leading a life. I was able to persuade my father and my sister Margaret to give me permission to get my inter-certificate at the school that is directly across the street from us. I wasn't fully lying when I told them I wanted to write about the poetry and the stories, and we never had enough time with John to study them, but my primary objective was not to become a nun or an elderly woman locked up in a facility by the time I was an old woman. Lady, work in a typing group, or be a "housewife" are all required occupations.

It was Sister Margaret's responsibility, in part, that I kept escaping; she shouldn't have purchased me that guitar in the first place. When he accompanied me to the store, I decided to buy an acoustic guitar with steel strings so that I could play like my older brother Joe.

57

While she was paying, I looked through the books on the shelves and found a Bob Dylan songbook that had pictures of how to play the chords and lyrics to the songs. I ordered her to get rid of it immediately. He assured me that he would find a teacher to come if that was what I want, and sure enough, one day a lovely lady by the name of Jeanette showed up. She had a very English accent, and as a result, she was neither square nor monotonous. She demonstrated for me how to determine, based on the drawings of the chords, what positions my fingers should be in. "To Ramona" was the first song I ever learnt to play on the guitar.

> Ramón, move in a little bit.
> Close your wet eyes with a gentle touch.
> The sharp pains caused by your grief
> It won't last if you keep your senses about you.
> The blooms that grace the city

Even yet, there are moments when breathing feels like dying, and it's pointless to try to make peace with death. However, I'm at a loss for words to explain why this is the case.

I barely stayed for maybe two or three classes before I started to leave before I realized what was happening. Being the child who witnessed the drama, flapping with painful fingers, and making music in the parks based on the pictures in my book were all traumatic experiences for me. I also make a point of flying in to see my mother on occasion. Once, they took me away from my mother's house and "got" me. After a period of twenty-four hours, he was obligated to return. There is nowhere else to go at this point. If I wasn't supposed to see my mother or if I had stolen things while I was AWOL (which, of course, I did), or if I needed to protect someone, like my brother's friend who let me spend the night on his office floor and would have consequently been killed if anyone found out, I would come back and lie a lot when I came back. On the few occasions that they didn't bring me back, I would come back and lie a lot when I came back.

Sister Margaret made an effort to free me from my mother's grasp while she was holding me. Because she was unable to communicate with me in any way throughout that task, it was her least favorite job. He never uttered a single word but rather just sobbed in complete silence while turning bright crimson. After some time, she would walk over to my side of the desk and hug me like one of her African babies so that I might cry into her pretty blue nun's blouse and wet her. This would make me laugh, and she would exclaim out loud Low, "Oh, Sinéady."

In the living room, she performed an African song called "Malika." I believe what he said was that it meant "angel." He enjoyed singing for fun. When she was a young nun, she spent several years in Africa in that continent. However, as a nun, they have the right to tell you where you should be, and they instructed her to return to Ireland. When she talks about it, her eyes get blue from the effort it takes to keep the tears from falling out of her eyes. It appears as though he is scanning the area outside the window for flying creatures. Her employment requires her to take care of depressed girls, and she herself falls into that category.

I was able to convince her to purchase a red parka for me from the punk clothing boutique No Romance, which is located on George's Street. Because I'm leaving, she decided to buy it. I've finished serving my time, and now, just like the song says, I'm going to get my life back. Permit me to restate that: I'm going to start living my life, and as a way to celebrate, she purchased me the parka. It is very satisfying. I have finally achieved the look of a true punk girl. I have a feeling that she will miss seeing me. She has a tendency to be a whiney brat.

Right now, I don't give a rat's behind about anyone other than myself, and I don't have a cold at all. I just want to get out of this place so that B. Can see me in my parka when we meet up later. That is the reason why I want it, and I insisted that Sister Margaret acquire it. The hope that I would see him again after moving here was the most painful thing to give up. He is wearing a parka that is green. It was stuffy in there with him, but it was the only place other than Granny's where I felt like I belonged.

Because I consented to attend boarding school, my parents have given me permission to depart. That will be the price. After spending the summer at my grandfather's house, I continue my education at a boarding school in Waterford. After that, i'll be able to visit my dad on every other weekend and during the times when school is out for the summer. According to my buddy, the price of two hard-boiled eggs on the train to Waterford is three pounds and ten pence. With that kind of money, you could easily purchase an entire brood of chickens.

There were a lot of wild children in Grianán. There was not even a square there. From them, I learnt a lot about the neighborhood I lived in and what other people thought of the people who lived there. I smoked more cigarettes and had fewer conversations with other punk females my age in the bathrooms than I did in the actual classes I was supposed to be attending. For those of us who did not take pleasure in life, smoking was the only thing that kept us going, and school played no role in our education at any point in our lives. It was a safe haven for those who needed it. I received a C in art, a D in other subjects, and the standard Es, Fs, and ngs in all of the other subjects. "no rating" stands for "NG." I really couldn't care less.

In the end, I can say that my time spent at Grianán was not without its positives. David, who was a nice young lad, and I fell in love with one other. He fit the stereotype of a true punk. He was completely prepared, with the hair, the safety pins, and everything else. You are not permitted to sit on any of our furniture, according to my father. I used to spend a lot of time at this guy's place. I was treated kindly by his mother, who was such a sweet and gentle person. Also, he. It's a lamb. Nobody could figure out what exactly had him so worked up because no one knew what the problem was. I was told by his mother that she was concerned about how he was doing. But we managed to have a good time together, and he didn't appear to be angry at any point. David and I were listening to Let's Dance side 1 as we made love while his parents were in the kitchen next to the living room. He was so ecstatic that his entire face, including his eyes, shone brightly like he was an astronaut, and he gave me the sweetest kiss.

Singing is something that I am already aware will cause me to become detached from other people.
Before I departed Grianán, I had the opportunity to sing at the wedding of my guitar instructor Jeanette. "Evergreen." The muscles in my knees shook. Paul Byrne, Jeanette's brother, is a member of a band named In Tua Nua and plays the drums for them. Ivan O'Shea,

the guitarist, and he presented me with a tape containing some music to listen to. Because they were seeking for a singer, they asked me if I would be willing to compose some words for them. I was able to sneak out of the convent on several Sundays thanks to Sister Margaret, and my friends escorted me to Eamonn Andrew's recording studio, where I performed my first song using reverb and headphones. The reverb is amazing; it makes the sound reminiscent of a church. It was really kind of Sister Margaret to give me permission to do it. My best guess is that it has something to do with the fact that they promised to pay me. It's not that I needed the money; I was just relieved that there was something else I could do except steal for a living. They decided to keep the song, which was titled "Take My Hand," but they decided that I was not old enough to be their singer. I was so envious of the girl who won the position that when I first heard her sing my lines, I wanted to cry because I was so angry with her. And not only was she stunningly attractive, but she also had a more impressive singing voice. It had the sound of a young child. It appeared to be a female voice. It is impossible for a youngster to be singing a song in which Death is the narrator.

I am unable to account for where it was obtained.

I SING TO THE SIREN

I AM DEVOTED TO MY STEPMOM. She is the kindest and gentlest woman in the entire world. When I say this, please understand that I mean it in a positive way: a woman will never advance your career. I have a sneaking suspicion that she is astute. Should she begin with any one of us, the remaining seven will anticipate the same treatment. She identifies as a Protestant. They offer a great deal more utility. They are innocent of the charges. She is not really concerned about it. They are not going to put you down or pick you up no matter how much you stare at them, blink at them, cry, kick, or whine to them about it. Ever. You have the choice to drown or swim. Therefore, I was aware that my mother had passed away when I saw her automobile heading toward me along Beechwood Avenue with my stepsister sobbing in the passenger seat.

I had just stepped out of my room in preparation to follow the weekly Sunday ritual of making the journey to my father's house on foot. C., my buddy who was the winner of the Halloween costume contest the year before despite the fact that she did not dress up for the holiday, now shares the room with me. It has been revealed that she is carrying on an affair with the lead vocalist of Fine Young Cannibals. It would appear that he is in good health, he is a young man, and he has invited her to tea, brunch, and dinner.

The night before, he had gone to bed as Kevin and I continued our conversation well into the night. Kevin used to be my boyfriend, but we're back to being the greatest of friends now. He is a conga player. He is a gentleman and very lovely to me. It is impossible for me to adequately express how kind and considerate he is to me. There is no relevance to whether or not we will be going out together. We're nothing more than the best of buddies regardless. As a result, we passed the evening of a Saturday brooding and chatting about nonsense.

We started talking about how any one of us may feel and respond in the event that one or both of our parents passed away. Another reason why I had a feeling when I spotted my stepmother's car was because of this. The fact that someone had told us anything the night before, and I was just finding out about it now, blew my mind.

John, my younger brother, had been in the vehicle at the time. In my mom's car, not in the one belonging to my stepmother. He was fortunate in that he did not sustain any physical injuries and was discharged from the hospital to be looked after by my father. He will be sixteen years old this year.

He had been seated in the trunk, and another man was driving with the other driver behind the wheel. To our great relief, he did not sustain any physical injuries either. After passing out, my brother regained consciousness at the hospital and was informed that his mother had passed away. When I arrived at my father's home, he was already there, dozing off in one of the beds. Or maybe I was sitting on a couch; I can't quite recall. It had been a very long time since any of us had seen him. He never abandoned the home of my mother. It was done by the rest of us.

The most serious offense in my mother's eyes was any of us, as a group of four, breaking into my stepmother's residence. My mother never for a moment gave any thought to the fact that betraying my brother was even remotely significant. But the concept of betraying her was like a crucifixion for him because he was so distraught over where he was in life at the time that he was and how much he needed her love.

Unfortuitously, my father and my younger brother have a terrible connection with one other. In about equal measures, both of my parents are to blame for this situation. They took advantage of my brother. It resulted in a tragic chain of events, for which my brother was held accountable while my father was the one who suffered the consequences of those events.

Since the official dissolution of my parents' marriage ten years ago, there had been a battle between my parents over a number of tangible possessions, all of which were pursued by my father with a great deal of vigor. This conflict had led to a war between my parents. Specific pieces of jewelry. Figurines crafted in Capodimonte. Pictures. Plus diverse other things. Some of the valuables were hidden in the attic, while others were stashed away in the bank. There had been a great number of attempts made, but none of them had been effective in removing the property from the custody of my mother.

A picture of them on their wedding day was propped up on the mantelpiece. My grandfather had taken it apart by breaking it in half and then reassembling it in the frame like a puzzle.

Because he bequeathed everything he owned on this land to my brothers, my father is powerless to intervene in decisions that concern his possessions. Even if she is no longer alive, the war goes on. Clever little whore. It was not because he cared about my brothers that he had given them his belongings; rather, he had done it so that we could win the war. To her, the four of us merely constituted a guarantee. That was the entirety of who we had ever been. At the very least, I have the impression that this is the case.

You have to wonder how on earth these folks ever managed to have enough sex to have four children when they truly detested one another as much as they did.

It was icy in appearance. Right adjacent to the church, on the brand-new road that's being constructed in Shankhill. She was in the car on her way to church. Either a bus or she skidded on the floor. I really have no idea. I'm not going to grill my brother about the specifics of the situation. She has passed away. And the four of us received orders from the undertaker, through my father, through my stepmother, along with fifty pounds, to go to Dunnes and buy a 'button down' dress for her to be buried in.

The four youngsters traveled to his residence. In disbelief We gave the whole thing a good shake like roosters. On the front lawn, we lit a biscuit tin on fire that contained a mountain's worth of Valium that we had poured in from every bottle we could locate of the drug. They report that she has been "eating and drinking" for a number of years now. Even a prescription wasn't necessary for me any longer. It was just handed to him by the chemist.

Putting it in the past tense is something that I am not yet accustomed to doing.

We were reduced to fits of uncontrollable laughter when in the Dunnes clothing store. Crying-laughing. The fact that the adorable young lady who was assisting us was unaware that we were looking for a dress that our mother would wear for the rest of her life made me find it absurdly humorous. We had to exert increasing effort to control our urge to urinate in response to his more insightful queries. The poor girl may have believed that we had escaped from the zoo when she asked about us.

I suppose that we did.

When everyone came up to us in church to shake hands, I felt a surge of anger that I couldn't control. This occurred the morning of the day that the funeral was to take place. We had reserved seats in the very front row. We had never come across these individuals during her lifetime. He was upset that they had not assisted us in any way. Or even she. He was clueless about who the most of them were. And the ones I met just served to infuriate me further. They were aware. Not the specifics here. But they were aware of it. And despite the fact that they hadn't helped in any way, they nevertheless came to offer their condolences, shake our hands, and express their sorrow at our misfortune. I almost asked, "Which specific loss?" but I refrained. On the other hand, I was already irritated with my older brother Joe, and I didn't want to make him any more so. On Easter Sunday, our family has a higher chance of resurrecting our mother from the grave than we do of regaining what we have actually misplaced. That we already are ourselves, many years in the past.

Last night, while looking up at the stars, I yelled at God. He referred to them as every horrible bastard under the sun till I became sick to my stomach. Saying hurtful words to me caused a lot of discomfort. It is not the first time that I have done anything like this.

He never speaks in response to questions. It took some time for me to come to terms with that. The first few days, I worked myself up into a rage. My assumption was that because he was silent, he was uninterested. Therefore, I would yell even louder until I could no longer yell and was forced to remain silent myself. I had the impression that, just like in all of the stories, you were meant to be able to hear His voice. I've come to realize that the reason why He is unable to speak is because He himself is crying quite a lot. Who can talk to you when you're in such a state?

My father was seen crying over my mother's body while we were at the funeral home. He kept repeating, "I'm sorry, Marie," throughout the conversation. That additionally infuriated me. Why do I feel sorry for you now and not earlier? Why did none of them say "I'm sorry" to the four of us when they screwed up? Why start a conflict and then feel compelled to apologize when someone loses their life? I escaped the funeral home by running away from there. Following the road past Glasthule and into Dun Laoghaire will bring you there. I don't think i'll ever be able to stop jogging. I'm not sure how i'll keep from ever getting furious. There will be no improvements made at this time.

The following day, when we were waiting for the hearses in the living room of my father's house, I made the decision to kill myself by smoking. I made the decision that I would start smoking when I was young and continue to smoke for as long as it took for my mother to give birth to me. Nothing else about the burial sticks out in my memory, save for the feet walking around the grave. I cast my eyes downward. It was all of us. Crying.

SISTERS

MY SISTER EIMEAR (her name is pronounced "Eeemer") is only fourteen months my senior. On the other hand, i've always looked up to her as both a mother and a sister.

When we were kids, we used to sleep in the same bed. There was a line that ran down the middle of what we imagined. And may God have mercy on any of us who have, whether by accident or on intent, stepped over the boundary. We'd be tearing each other to shreds with our fists and feet. As a couple of guys, we engaged in a significant amount of that activity.

However, the moment the proverbial crap struck the fan, Éimear would immediately turn into mother mode. To give you an example, she and I got into a disagreement on Christmas morning at my father's house, where we shared a room with two single beds. During the fight, she trampled on my chocolate Santa, so it's no surprise that I kicked him in the back savagely and rushed out the door, with her chasing after me. Before running away and falling to the ground wailing in agony, I merely damaged my ankle. The conversation was put on hold as quickly as it had begun as Éimear dropped to the ground next to me and exclaimed, "Oh my gosh, are you okay?" She has a Love for Me. I have no idea why that is. However, she does.

It was awful having to share that bedroom in my father's house with her for one reason in particular: she was head over heels in love with Barry Manilow. Therefore, the wall on her side of the room was covered with enormous posters of him, whereas the wall on my was covered with posters of Siouxsie and the Banshees. If my posters horrified her into the night as much as it scared me to talk about Manilow in romantic terms, then I think that each of us woke up in hell. I imagine that my posters scared her into the night.

Previously, she had feelings for Daniel Boone but they eventually ended their relationship. Now that's something I could get behind. Not so with Manilow though. But, of course, she and I have never preferred the same kind of men, which is a blessing from God. Punks and bad lads are cool in my book. She is attracted to gentlemen who are uninteresting.

He was never in problems with our mother or our father. Which really got under my skin. He never managed to stay out of mischief. Because she was unable to differentiate between our voices, she would occasionally refer to my father as Éimear. I was able to predict the punishments that awaited Sinéad when she returned to her house because of her behavior.

Because of the Santa experience, we still enjoy breaking chocolate, therefore every year at Christmas we stomp on a few of chocolate Santas, and every Easter we shatter some lovely chocolate chickens with a hammer. Both of these traditions began because of the Santa episode. During the time that she was going through a breakup, we established that tradition. It was Easter, and, well, someone had given someone a chocolate chicken in a basket, so I just handed her a hammer when she started screaming in my kitchen. As she shattered the object into a million pieces, she couldn't help but giggle through her tears.

Although Éimear was never in any legal trouble, this does not mean that she was incapable of getting into scrapes. The difference is that she was never apprehended in the same way that I was. He held the position of prefect at his school. He made my life and the lives of my little group, who were all considered to be "bad" females, a living misery. When she was chasing after us, I would stop what I was doing, make a square shape with my hand, and then refer to it as a square. It used to drive her absolutely bonkers. On the other hand, I'm more round than she is. And that makes me envious. I have a deep-seated desire to have straight hair. Being square-oval is an uncomfortable shape to be in.

She went on to earn a doctorate in art history. Extremely astute. And she is not one to put up with fools for one second. A number of years ago, he operated a storefront where he sold his own exquisite paintings to customers. He did not open the shop's door for anyone. A tremendous door, and he was successful in putting all of the hinges together. And she weighs only fifty percent of what I do. She is convinced that she is obese at all times. However, she is not in any way.

The color of his hair, which is red, and his level of confidence are two ways in which he is distinct from me. I do not possess either of them. She forces me to repeat positive affirmations such as, "I'm loving. I am charitable. Look in the mirror and say things like, "I love and accept myself," etc. It isn't working, but just being in her presence improves the way I feel about myself. Because he enjoys spending time with me, and he does not enjoy spending time with anyone who does not love him. There is no evidence of any mental disorder in her. She has never given me any trouble in the rear end. She is not challenging or excessively emotional like I can be. She is not vengeful in the same way that I am. She does not exhibit any negative tendencies. It is possible to remove yourself from an abusive situation without becoming abusive yourself. I admire her in such qualities and aspire to have them myself. God is aware that I'm putting some effort into it.

Recently, he paid a visit to me in the hospital while I was there. He said "I love you" as he led me by the hand into the garden that was adjacent to the hospital where I was staying. It was as if we had suddenly been transported back to our younger selves. When we were younger, we often went on adventures in Dublin together, exploring places like Moore Street and Parnell Street. We had borrowed money from some random people, and we were going to spend it at the Kingfisher chip shop. We said to them that we needed the money to buy a ticket for the bus back home. The truth of the matter is that we were making every effort to stay away from home. (During this time, we were residing with our mother). Anything to get us out of the house, because nothing good ever happened when we were there. On certain evenings, we would ride the bus all the way to its last destination, wait there, and then ride it back home in the hopes that Mom would be asleep when we got there. We were a weird mix: youngsters from middle-class families who were begging while wearing soiled clothes that hadn't been washed in years. We were skilled in begging because we were forced to do so in order to avoid starvation. We would weep and bury our hockey sticks inside the school during the summer, when all of the other children couldn't wait to get out of school and go home. We were well aware that we were in for several weeks of bloody conflict. The other children eagerly anticipated weeks filled with happiness, which made their mothers smile. The one we had was drooling profusely. No one to save us can be found. Not even a breather Only the absolute certainty of impending death.

ANY DREAM WILL DO

MY BROTHER IN LAW JOSEPH and I have a relationship that is quite similar to the one I have with my father in the sense that the only time we can get along is when we discuss music. My brother doesn't like me very often, but when he does, I feel special. Because I'm a pain in the neck and I let my feelings get the best of me. But when we were younger, he was a role model for me to look up to. In an effort to imitate the coolness of him, he used to carry around his empty guitar box. In spite of the fact that he went through a period in which he desired to become a priest, he eventually settled on a career in writing instead. In addition, he is the author of Redemption Falls, which happens to be one of my top two favorite books of all time (the other book, by Neil Jordan, is called Mistaken).

Since I was eighteen years old and our mother passed away, we have probably only spent a total of one hour together. Children who have been abused often find it difficult to be around one another. Indicators and prompts for action. Plus, I may have given in to him a little bit too frequently. In addition to that, he lost his temper with me way too frequently. We, the O'Connors, are a grumpy family. It's a shame, in all honesty. They did not provide us with an example demonstrating that blood has a greater viscosity than water. It seems certain to me that water, and not blood, circulates through our veins.

Joe is proficient on the guitar. Although he claims that he isn't a good player, he actually is. My older brother is the drummer in the family, and my younger sister plays the harp. It has always occurred to me that it would be hilarious to record an album with them and give it the title Fuck the Corrs. However, the battles would have made Noel and Liam Gallagher appear to be cowards in comparison.

It's hilarious, Joe, my older brother. Pants is slang for "pissingly funny." I think about him and miss him often. And I am sorry about that. Myself because of the great distance that separates us. But he is still someone I look up to. And to the depths of my being, I adore him.

JUAN, I LOVE YOU

John, who is my younger brother, was born two years after I did. He was in trouble a lot from my mum. The evenings in which I heard him plead for mercy (at his command), but I was unable to save him played a significant role in the development of my activist tendencies and my difficulty controlling my wrath. I was unable to save it. I was unable to shield him from harm. I literally couldn't move a muscle as I tried to make my way from my room to his. My entire life, I have harbored resentment toward my mother. However, I relocated it. I was incapable of admitting that she was the reason for my anger, so I took it out on everyone else instead. And he destroyed the majority of the relationships I had.

If I could travel through time and crush my mother under my feet or put her in jail, I most certainly would. But I am unable to. The events that transpired in our lives did not allow John and I to emerge as well adjusted as my older brothers did. Self-esteem building is not taught to us in the same way as it was to Joe and Éimear. Our only education consisted of our mother lecturing us about how much of a disaster we were in her life. She embarrassed John in front of the rest of us, and then she embarrassed the rest of us in front of John. I lied to him on numerous occasions and told him that I was responsible for something that John was being punished for, all in an effort to prevent him from hitting John. Instead, he would be the one to suffer the blows.

I am very aware that Éimear has the same feelings toward me. It was painful for her that she could not save me. The same way that I was hurt by the fact that I couldn't save John.

When John and I were both in our teenage years, we went together to the theater to watch the scary movie Halloween. The perpetrator of the crime sported a hockey goalie mask in white. Then John gave chase to me the entire length of O'Connell Street while wearing his white motorbike helmet in an inverted position. I'll never understand how it managed to avoid colliding with anything else. It gave me the creeps to say the least.

During a pretend battle we were having, I bit his nose. The sneaky scoundrel blew his nose into my mouth.

The truth is that our family is somewhat disorganized. We don't even belong in the same category as the word "family." There must be some solace in those words. However, it is not. This is an excruciating and venomous word. Separate the chambers of the heart. And the fact that it is now impossible to reverse course and try something else adds insult to injury.

ABOUT MY DAD

When I was around fifteen years old, I made several attempts to acquire some hash, but I was never successful. Mostly because the person to whom I handed the five dollars passed away. Also, my father was not the one who was responsible for his death.

My stepfather was aware that the man was up to no good because he was my stepsister's boyfriend. One night, a creep was watching my stepsister's front door from the path that leads to my father's front garden. He peered over the hedge and waited for her to come out. My grandfather kept an eye on him and punched him in the side of the head after luring him into the garden with comments like "She'll be out in a minute, come in." After my grandfather had him on the ground, he continued to spy on him. He was slender despite his height. Both my father and I are exactly five feet and four inches tall.

Dude had the utter stupidity (this is an Anglo-Irish word for the kind of stupidity that would have had Bill Clinton in the Oval Office with a cigar and Monica Lewinsky) to come back another night assuming that my father was out. My younger brother was at an age where he could legally own a tricycle at the time. Outside the front door, he was lounging on the itty-bitty porch that was covered in red tiles. My grandfather grabbed the tricycle as soon as he saw the other individual, hurried with it to the front door, jumped on it, and began to pursue the other individual down the road. As he pedaled, his knees came dangerously close to making contact with his face. The poor man raced for his life for kilometers, glancing back over his shoulder every few seconds with such a look of pure fear on his face that you would have thought Freddy Krueger was after him.

When my older brother was younger, he attended a school where every morning a dog would make fun of him. After a few weeks had passed with no discernible change in the circumstances, my father and my brother set out to locate the dog. Joe is met with an angry growl from the dog. Francis Street is being kicked by my father. Joe was never in danger of being attacked by the dog again. You do not want to upset my paternal grandfather. I suppose I'm similar to him.

When my sister and I were approximately five and six years old, respectively, there was a day when we cornered a poor girl at school who had the audacity to claim that her father was more gorgeous than ours. My sister and I were furious about this. We didn't want our father's gibberish, so we forced him to take it back, despite the fact that our father was the most attractive man in the world. It's not like we were going to injure her, and we didn't make any explicit threats or anything; instead, we simply stated our full rejection of her appraisal of the situation and then towered over her in silence until she backed down. It's not like we were going to hurt her, and we didn't make any specific threats or anything. After the fact, we shared with our father how pleased we were to report that his honor and reputation had been preserved.

If I haven't done so already, I feel obligated to comment on the remarkable and humbling humility exhibited by my father. Which I am hoping to receive at least a drop or two of. Naturally, when he reached the age of eighty-two, he took his retirement from the field of building engineering. Nevertheless, it helps lift me up whenever I'm feeling low. When I'm feeling down, it helps me feel like I can conquer the world again. I have a lot of love for him, and I feel terrible that I didn't communicate with him when he was younger because I thought he was too naive. I would strongly encourage any young man to avoid make the same mistakes I did. Time passes quickly, and there is no way to bring it back once it has passed.

However, the fact that we are currently together is the most wonderful thing that has ever happened to either of us in our lives.

POEM OF MY YOUTH

If you dance with me, the child who has been talking will stop talking. I did not wake you up.

Aside from that, you won't need dreams while you sleep with me because i'll keep you awake.

If you are at a loss as to who to be, you can always be me.

I'm the one who offered my assistance, but I don't appreciate being pigeonholed.

Some people refer to me as music, while others name me the great absolver. I sat with her when she believed I was a hazy spirit, and I claimed her as my own because I love her.

Because? A delicate young lady, we don't want to risk losing her.

Faith on the level that she possessed is extremely rare.

I heeded her plea for assistance when she made the call.

She utters the words, "I just want to vanish."

I encircled her tiny waist with both of my hands.

I threw her around and whirled her all over the place, and the colors black, green, and red shone on my face.

When the light was directed at her, she vanished into the void.

THE SECOND PART

WHO ARE YOU?

THE BEST DAY OF MY LIFE WAS THE DAY THAT I LEFT IRELAND FOR THE FIRST TIME, and every other day that I left Ireland was the next best day of my life.

It turned out that there was someone up there who wanted me, so in 1985, about a fortnight or so after I buried my mother (don't worry, we made sure she was dead first), Ensign Records contacted me via a guy named Ciaran Owens. Who I met while singing with Ton Ton Macoute, a band I joined the previous summer. Ensign Records wanted to know if I was interested in recording with them. Colm Farrelly, the leader of the band and bassist, believed that he was a witch, thus he chose a horrific name for the band, which was based on the Haitian secret police.

In Ireland's one and only music magazine, Hot Press, I placed an advertisement introducing myself as a singer who was interested in joining a band. I did auditions in people's garages and living rooms all around the Dublin suburbs, and in the end, I decided to go with Ton Ton since it didn't appear likely to be a typical situation musically speaking, while everyone else had been mad. The absolute deal-sealer that is Colm.

In addition to this, he gave his approval for us to perform some of my songs, although the other bands did not. If I had chosen one of the other bands, they would have made me sing "Summertime" for the rest of my life, and I would have preferred to have my eyes gouged out instead.

Approximately one year was spent on Ton Ton. Nigel Grainge, a leading record executive, and Chris Hill, of the Ensign, were interested in finding performers in Ireland due to the success that Ireland had previously had with the Boomtown Rats and Thin Lizzy. Ciaran Owens was one of the individuals they turned to when they needed guidance on what was and was not considered fashionable in the city. They had attended one of our concerts thanks to him around six months previously.

Now they had called me after discovering my whereabouts through Ciaran's investigation. They informed me that they wanted me to travel to London to do some demos with Karl Wallinger from the Waterboys, and they inquired as to when I would be available to do so. They told me that they were only interested in me and not the band, which was OK with me because only a few weeks before, we had discovered that Colm had been keeping all of the money that we earned for him, which led to the dissolution of the band.

I was able to get on an aircraft forty-eight hours after the Ensign had phoned me thanks to the nice manager of the restaurant where I worked, the Bad Ass Café in Dublin. All of the servers there wore T-shirts, and the management was kind enough to offer me one hundred pounds to help me get on the plane. Ones that were white and stated "NICE ASS PIZZA." (I'm not making this up; it wasn't until I was twenty-eight that I had any genuine comprehension of what it meant.)

I did demos of four songs with Karl, and in the end, three of those songs were used on my debut album, titled "The Lion and the Cobra." The first was a song that I had written the year before titled "Drink Before the War." It was about a principal that I had who despised the fact that I made music and campaigned for my father to not let me take my guitar to boarding school, despite the fact that all he could do was produce music. The song was about how my principal was constipated and how he hated it when I played music. I used to light up right outside his door in an effort to provoke him into kicking me out as a form of retaliation for his opposition to the music I was playing. It was never successful. When I arrived at school one morning, he reprimanded me in front of the whole assembly. He was a snob with a heart of stone. "If you're going to make music," he grumbled through his superior nose, "you're going to spend the rest of your life going out the back door." Pronounce the final two syllables as though their literal meaning were "dog shit," with the emphasis on the first word. I had no idea that getting in through the back door was the objective of the game. In his mind, having fun was the most dangerous of all crimes.

There was a reason I was so angry: one of my instructors, a man with a beautifully black beard and a love of music whose name was Joe Falvey, had a buddy who had a recording studio in Cork, which was quite a distance from Waterford, where our school was located. This friend of Joe Falvey's had a recording studio in Cork. Since my friend Jeremy and I had been playing guitars on the street in Waterford and had gained a decent amount of notoriety for ourselves, Mr. Falvey had taken us to Cork on multiple occasions to record throughout the night before sending us back to school undetected. And then we are all in a bind.

Busking was something that Jeremy and I had done on the weekends as well as after school. Even before that, we had been doing concerts in a tavern that was nearby. Therefore, we weren't putting any effort into our academic pursuits at all. There was no way for us to even attempt it. Mr. Falvey had the same response. However, the director was having none of it. We were bringing shame and ridicule upon the school with our rock and roll antics.

I awoke on a Friday morning to find that the first lesson that day was double home economics. This came after a few weeks during which I had avoided being expelled. I had no intention of ever becoming a stay-at-home mom. What I had seen of him left a bad impression on me. I couldn't stand being in the kitchen. In addition to that, I had plans to have sexual encounters with multiple men.

That morning, I requested my good friend Hugh to accompany me to the train station so that I could travel back to Dublin. I can't recall if he drove or how we got to the station, but once we arrived, he assisted me in gathering my belongings and escorting me to the train.

I traveled to Colm's residence. Even though he was an older man than the rest of us in Ton Ton Macoute, he still lived with his mother, who was also an older person. I asked him for some money and remained with him for a few nights before moving on to a place in Dublin known as Dolphin's Barn, where I rented a room.

I went approximately a week without getting in touch with my dad. When I did, he didn't seem to be bothered by it. He became aware of the fact that he had complete control over my thoughts. And in addition to that, I started playing in a band. He was astute; he provided me with two hundred pounds a month, which was precisely enough to pay my rent and no more, so that I could not laze around and not work if I needed to eat or pay my bills. He knew that this would force me to get a job. Not that I would have done it anyhow even if I had the chance. However, it was really astute.

The person who lived in the room above was a bricklayer and was a really large man. At one point, I required a loan of twenty pounds from him. Because I was late with my payment, he broke into my room while I was gone and stole everything I owned from there. Included in that was a flute that had been a gift from my good friend Barbara. I relocated.

The band did nothing but practice during the day and every day, with the exception of working hours, and also throughout the night for the few bar gigs and talent shows that we participated in. My workplace was located only down the street from the location where we had a space on the upper floor of an old building on Crown Alley. I ate as much pizza as I possibly could. And every single cook I could possibly woo. Therefore, I sang to the best of my ability.

In addition to that, I found work as a kissogram model. Someone would have to pay me twenty-five pounds for the privilege of dressing up as a French maid, reciting a meaningless poetry with a terrible French accent, and placing a pair of frilly French underwear on the head of some unfortunate individual. Despite the fact that the work was called "Kisses," there were never any actual kisses because it took place in Ireland.

They handed over six pounds out of the total amount of twenty-five. My good friend Barbara was married to Steve Wickham, a violinist for the bands In Tua Nua and the Waterboys. She was the one who gave me the flute that was later stolen. Because she was feeling a little bit bored, she approached me one day and inquired as to whether or not she could also be a kissogram girl. She was an American from Atlanta, which meant that she was more courageous than I was; in addition, she was stunning, vivacious, and blonde. She was made to wear a bikini that had chewable balloons attached to her bra and pantyhose by the man who controlled the company, who went to great lengths to take advantage of the situation and went by the name of Hot Lips.

I can't help but feel a little green with envy. But after that, I'd change into my favorite outfit, which was called "the naughty nun." It consisted of a full head-to-toe habit in the front, but nothing from the waist down in the rear. I also wore fishnet stockings and stilettos.

It felt so awful, but at the same time it felt so right.

I believe that out of all the kissogram girls, I was the worst ever. I used to be quite timid. And the poems, which were written by the guy who headed the company, were awful to the point of being embarrassing. I would get the shivers just reading them, and I would bolt as soon as I heard them pronounced.

The gentleman who managed the business was likewise skilled in the art of making gorillagrams and Tarzans for the ladies. It appeared as though he resided in a building that had formerly served as a children's home run by priests. At this time, the residence was occupied by a senior priest as well as a number of younger guys. In the glass arch that was located above the entranceway was a sizeable statue of a Virgin Mary with a light blue and white color scheme. The guy drove an automobile that was crimson all over, including the lips on the hood. Once upon a time, while driving through Deansgrange Cemetery in search of my mother's grave, the Lord have mercy on us, he was dressed as a gorilla, and I was dressed as a French maid, and we were giggling like fools the entire time.

"Just Like U Said It Would B" was the following song that I demoed for Ensign that ended up being included on my first album. Steve Wickham was the musician who contributed to this track. It was about a lesson that I had received from a certain preacher on the art of praying Psalm 91 and the benefits that it may produce, and the title of my album was drawn from that passage.

Then there was the song "Never Get Old," which was another one that she had composed in school. It was about a very shy kid that all of the females in the class had a crush on in secret. He kept a hawk as a pet. Once, he showed me around the area by taking me to the field and guiding me around. He gave me permission to wear his leather glove so that I could feed the bird uncooked pieces of meat. He was a young man with a really kind and generous spirit.

I was given a record deal after listening to the demos, and on August 5, 1985, I accepted the offer and signed the contract. The Ensign attorney had dispatched me to grovel and beg for permission to let him negotiate a better deal for me. However, I wasn't willing to take any chances. I had no complaints at all. He was just interested in leaving Ireland and establishing himself as a financially independent person as soon as possible, and he wasn't going to wait for another opportunity. I agreed to the terms of seven points, which state that you would receive a payment equal to seven percent of the revenue generated by the sale of your recordings, and that seven percent will be used to cover the costs of recording, promoting, and touring.

It was the lawyer's responsibility to go through the entire contract with me and make sure I understood everything. On the other hand, I was only eighteen at the time, and when you're just eighteen, contracts are incredibly dull. Just before my eyes finally started to glaze over, he told me, in all seriousness, about a condition that indicated that the terms of my contract would apply on the moon if and/or when the records could be released on the moon. He said this right before my eyes finally started to glaze over. When he asked me if I understood this, I immediately nodded off to sleep.

After that, the only thing that was going through my mind was a picture of a lone, black and white flag representing the United States of America waving on the moon. He was thinking that rather than receiving records that would make his loneliness worse because no one would be there to wipe his tears when he heard the This Mortal Coil version, he would prefer to return home and live on Earth in color, eating hamburgers and hot dogs. He would do this rather than receive songs that would make him feel even more alone. The song is addressed to the mermaid.

Pete Townshend was on my flight the day I left Ireland for real, which was a few weeks prior to when we signed the contract. In those days, Aer Lingus flights were similar to trains in that they had seats arranged in pairs that faced each other. He was seated in the seat directly opposite mine. Either The Who held a show in Ireland, or he went to some enormous concert there, but both of these possibilities are possible. When I boarded the plane, I had already made up my mind that I would not even turn around to look out the window when we were taking off. As we ascended into the air, I kept my attention fixed on Townshend's face because I interpreted his presence as validation that I had made the correct decision. I detested my time spent in Dublin. Everything brought up fond memories of my mom. The shops were stuffed with caps that she would have adored wearing but that you could never offer her at this point in time.

At Heathrow, there were usually two men in suits from Special Branch waiting at the end of the gangplank as you exited the plane from Ireland. One would be on the left, and the other would be on the right. They would be standing behind black podiums just before you entered the baggage claim area. Only guys were stopped, and the ones they were looking for had long hair and scruffy beards. This is due to the fact that during the early 1980s, there was a time when people participating in hunger strikes in Northern Ireland were hairy, as was everyone else in the IRA. Because they were continually shouting, the opposing side did not have a beard of any kind, and they also did not have very much hair. Since as far back as I can remember, everyone in that place had been murdering one another, I watched it happen. It looked terrible on the TV, with flames and blood and people of all ages, including toddlers and the elderly, wailing in the streets. And feces all over the walls of the prison, along with skeletal inmates with sunken eyes whose caskets were so light that even a kid could have carried them. And gunmen were at funerals, as well as men being ripped from cars and executed there. In spite of everything, Margaret Thatcher's hair was always styled in a way that was absolutely flawless.

During the approximately one month that passed before I finally left Ireland, I traveled to London on one or two occasions. In the meanwhile, an expert in Irish music accounting called me at my apartment in Dublin to offer his services. I was completely unfamiliar with him and any profession even somewhat related to accounting. Oh, he adds, "you'll need someone to manage your money for you, and i've got the ideal manager for you." In addition, he says, "i've got the ideal manager for you." Fachtna o'Ceallaigh, a former member of the Boomtown Rats management team.

In point of fact, I first encountered Fachtna when I was just thirteen years old, which was five years earlier. It happened one day in the lobby of Dublin's Four Courts building while the Rats were being banned from playing live in Dublin at the time. There was a hearing in the case of the Rats on the same day as there was a hearing in the case involving my parents.

When my brother Joseph saw Fachtna strolling down the hallway toward the front door to go outside for a smoke, he was so excited that he leaped up to get an autograph from him. The only thing he said to me when he approached me with Fachtna and introduced her was, "This is my little sister." I feel as though our handshake took place no more than thirty minutes ago when I think about it.

Before I left Ireland for good, I had two meetings with the accountant, during which he drove me completely insane by insisting that "we should go through all this" (the specifics of my record and publishing deals) with my father before I signed anything. During those sessions, I ultimately left Ireland. Despite this, I had a great deal of respect for the accountant; I found that I had to remind him again and over, each time in a little higher voice, that I was eighteen, thank you very much, and that it was no longer my father's responsibility, and that the fact that I was a woman didn't mean that I wasn't just because I was a woman. Despite this, I had a lot of respect for the accountant. That is something that I would have done. When my attorney took the time to sit down with me and clarify the contracts, I had no trouble understanding what they said. He misinterpreted my anger for concern that my father wouldn't have to worry about me, but in reality, I was very relieved. In point of fact, my grandmother advised me on multiple occasions that a lady should never discuss her financial situation with any of her male relatives.

The second time I met Fachtna o Ceallaigh, we were in a restaurant on Marylebone High Street in London, and we shook hands as I was settling into a rickety chair across from him in the restaurant. I tried to jog her memory by pointing out that we'd met in the past, but of course she couldn't recall it even though she was cutting through the egg yolks with the tip of her knife.

After I had returned to Dublin, he sent me a card with a note written in what appeared to be a beautiful Irish handwriting, in which he expressed his happiness at having the opportunity to meet me. I was confident that I would have success in the music industry, and I stressed to me the need of staying true to who I am no matter what others in the industry expect of me to be. It hadn't occurred to me that it might be anything other, but seeing an adult defend the right, for instance, not to pluck your eyebrows for a picture shoot, was helpful. Or the privilege of choosing whether or not to wear a blouse in the presence of a certain European gentleman who was the photographer. (This, after one had been naive enough to fall for the trap of taking off his top in the first place because said photographer had framed it as a dare. He had asked an Irish woman, "Would you mind taking off your top?" before they began their conversation. I am sorry to have to say this, but Fuck you for asking.)

During my first few months in London, I resided at my Aunt Martha's house in South London. It was then that I was introduced to my two male cousins. One of them pretended to be a female but in reality he was a heterosexual guy with long red hair dye and he was dressed as a feminine. The other one was the coolest other guy in the entire world, and he had short hair that was curly and blonde. They took me out partying and shopping on the King's Road for a lycra dress in a peach color. We went to his mother's lawn to watch Live Aid. We went to Clacton-on-Sea for an all-night concert by Doctor and the Medics, and I ended myself dozing off with my head resting dangerously close to a massive speaker. My cousin who dresses as a girl took me to Kensington Market, where I found a plethora of men's size 12 patent leather stilettos. My cousin dresses as a girl. It was officially determined that England was the largest country in the globe.

In addition to this, I met my first spiritual guide.

When I was sitting with folks I had only met once or twice prior to becoming eighteen, I would see the inside of their homes in my thoughts. This continued until I became twenty-one. I saw the rugs, the walls, the pictures on the walls, the tiny knickknacks on the nightstands, the colors of the pots and pans, the cache of private letters, and everything else there was to see. It appeared as though he was simply floating through his home.

I couldn't help but inquire with everyone was present about the veracity of what they claimed to be seeing, and every time, they confirmed my suspicions. Despite the fact that I had never set foot in the previous Ensign

Records office, I was able to provide a description of it when I met Chris Hill and Nigel Grainge. I didn't give much thought to the experience of seeing objects; I just accepted it as normal. But people looked at me as if I thought I should have something important to say them, and I didn't; I got tired of failing them because of how they looked at me. I had a strong need to understand what was going on below it all so that I could put a stop to it.

Psychic research was something that Aunt Martha and her sisters were all interested in. I informed him of what was going on, and he referred me to a friend of his, a pastor at the Greenwich Baptist Church who was also a medium and who instructed other people in the art of practicing mediumship. He was forty-seven years old. I told him that I wanted to learn how to shut off the part of myself that was roaming about inside other people without their permission. I wanted to learn how to do this so that I could stop being a parasite.

The problem was that they were not being true to themselves when it occurred, and that was the root of the problem.

Psalm 91 was the first thing I did each day as part of my training, and I said it aloud.

He who lives in the protection of the Most High, he will sleep in the shade of the Most High.

In reference to the Lord, I will proclaim, "He is my refuge and my fortress; he is my God, and I put my trust in him."

You can rest assured that he will save you from the terrible plague and the hunter's trap.

He will protect you by surrounding you with his feathers, and you will take shelter beneath his wings;

the faithfulness of God will serve as both your shield and your bulwark.

You will not be afraid of the dread that comes with the night, the arrow that flies during the day, the pestilence that stalks in the darkness, or the plague that destroys during the middle of the day.

You might have a thousand people fall by your side or ten thousand people fall by your right hand, but it still won't come anywhere near you.

You won't be able to do much more than watch the wicked get their just desserts in front of your very eyes.

If you declare, "The Lord is my refuge," and make the Most High your home place, then no harm will come near you, and no catastrophe will occur anywhere near your business.

For he will send his angels around you to keep you in all your ways; they will pull you up in their hands so that you do not trip over your foot when it is on stone.

You will tread the enormous lion and the serpent under your feet, and you will step on the lion and the cobra.

"Because he loves me," declares the Lord, "I will rescue him; I will protect him, for acknowledging my name."

He will come to me for help, and I will come to him in his time of need. I will save him from his predicament, and I will respect him.

I will put an end to it with a long life, and I will show him the way to salvation."

One evening, as I was sitting in my room, I noticed a person reflected in the glass cabinet. This person was wearing a black hood that was adorned with two gold bands around the edges. After then, the lights began flashing on and off, and I immediately fled the area in complete terror. The preacher told me that I missed an important message and that I should have stayed because I was supposed to receive it. I responded with a negative and stated that I did not wish to get any communications from anyone living in the neighborhood.

After I had completed my transfer to London and moved out of my aunt's house, the minister professed his everlasting love for me, and we had a relationship that was somewhat sexual in nature. When my aunt found out about this, it did not set well with her. Not only was the minister already married, but I think she loved him as well. This did not sit well with her. I was raging inside. In all honesty, she has never truly gotten past it. Years later, when I went to a family reunion with the father of one of my sons, she pointed at it and then on her chest while looking at me across the dance floor and muttering quietly, "i'll have it, i'll have it."

Since I was a child and an idiot at the time, the minister had managed to convince me that his wife could not comprehend him. I was his one and only love and everything else. After some time had passed, I came to the conclusion that I was being duped into believing nonsense. I was like Whitney Houston from the song Houston, holding all of my love in like a total jerk while I was sitting alone until our weekly one-hour visit. I wasn't dating anybody else either. I quickly realized my mistake and stopped underestimating him.

After leaving my aunt's house, the minister made his way to the flat in Lewisham that he had rented later that same evening. He was stuck with a faulty vacuum cleaner that his wife had no use for anymore. I was thinking that it would be a nice gift for me. He had the audacity to confess to her that he was acquainted with a person who might love him.

As I watched him walk to his car from the sixth-floor balcony of my apartment building, I considered throwing it on his head.

I went out and purchased a Fiat Bambino in the color yellow for myself. That means you may get behind the wheel of a car in England with just a provisional license. In all of my years, I had never been instructed in anything. When I got into the automobile, it was really late in the evening, and I was involved in an accident. I made a phone call to the minister and explained the situation: "I'm hurt, I crashed my car, will you come and get me?" He said that he wouldn't and wouldn't allow anyone else to see it with me since he didn't want anyone else to see it. I never spoke to him again after that.

In point of fact, he was in a lot of pain. I managed to rotate my pelvis. He was struck by a car going full speed on the driver's side of the vehicle. Even now, I still have to get dressed up occasionally. The movement on the right side does not behave as expected. Walk in good spirits. Stride in the manner of Charlie Chaplin. I couldn't remember the last time I walked like this.

SETTLING IN

AROUND EIGHT MILLION PEOPLE CALL THE CITY OF LONDON home at any given time. That's enough people to double Ireland's overall population! For the same reason that infinity is terrifying, I find that to be a little bit unsettling. It is much too large. The width of the Liffey is one hundred times smaller than that of the Thames.

The night sky is never devoid of the twinkling lights of passing aircraft. There is a constant influx of aircraft from every corner of the globe. Ireland is never a stop for airplanes that are en route to or from somewhere else. The precise moment that anyone who has had the intelligence to go needs to return for fear of becoming a bad son or daughter, unless there are Irish planes ferrying Irish in and out of the nation for growing quantities of money towards Christmas. Unless there are Irish planes ferrying Irish in and out of the country for increasing amounts of money towards Christmas.

I detest the Christmas season. My spirit hurts so badly it feels as if someone has stabbed a tree into the center of my chest.

My cousins and my aunt are the only relatives I have in London; the only other people I know there are Chris and Nigel from Ensign and Fachtna, my manager.

The majority of my time is spent at Chris's residence. He treats me with a lot of consideration and courtesy. He is quite concerned about my well-being. I have a sneaking suspicion that he has a crush on me, but he is happily married to a great woman whom he would never disobey.

Nigel gave me two cassettes with songs by Van Morrison to listen to. It's the first time i've ever heard it. He gives off the impression of being one of those Tibetan monks who uses the power of his voice to heal. At some university on the other side of the veil, he seduces me. It's not his words that are important; it's what he does with the sounds they make. It has brought me to the place where I should be studying. I saw breathtaking stone structures, some of which have golden buttresses.

The sitting room in my apartment is located at the front of the building and has a view of Hither Green Lane. A compact kitchen and a bedroom are located right next to it. It is located directly over an Indian supermarket. I've made some good friends there; one of them has a skinny son who's about my age and is interested in music. The folks there are friendly to me. We had no romantic feelings for one another; our relationship was strictly platonic. We would just sit there and chat like old friends. He did not own a record player, although I did. He could enjoy a cigarette without fear of his mother and father's disapproval.

He was a child with a high degree of sensitivity. His father made the decision at some point that he needed to toughen up, and as a result, he coerced him into joining the paratroopers. The poor creature scurried frantically up my stairs in a panic, looking terrified the whole time and crying, "What am I going to do?" There was nothing that any of us could do to change the situation. Because of what his father had done, he was forced to leave the country the following day.

After almost two weeks had passed, I was awakened by the sound of my doorbell. I went to check on who might be there, and it turned out to be him! He was always trying to escape. The fact that he was so courageous made me feel quite proud. His expression radiated complete and utter bewilderment. Not just because of what she had been subjected to over the previous two weeks—screaming, pushups, and everything else that is commonplace and can be seen on television—but also because she had disobeyed her father.

Because she was terrified to go home, she stayed with me and slept on my couch for a week. During that time, I went downstairs every day and bought the food that we were going to eat, conversing with her parents while being cautious not to mention her kid. During that period, she ate the meal that I made for us, but she didn't eat any of it. (and they never once discussed it), in that case I would pull back. After he fled the scene and went into hiding, I never had another word from him. After that, I didn't remain a resident of Hither Green Lane for very long.

Songs are the occupation of a lonely person; they are ghosts. Although I feel lonely, I am creating songs for my first album, and songs are the occupation of a lonely person. When my CD is finally out, I'm going to become a wandering "ghost delivery girl." There will be countless opportunities to say farewell. There is no way that I could object to that.

"Troya" is the name of a song that I created, and it's about both my mother and the pastor. The vocal demo was recorded at Chris's place by me. I sent him to wait outside the door in the lobby. When I opened the door for him, he acted really surprised. According to him, he had never heard anything quite like it or at such a high volume. It forced me to perform the action repeatedly in succession.

On Sundays when there are no shoppers on Fleet Street, I indulge my covert desire to contribute to the local press by taking a stroll along the street. Not about current events or even music, but rather about literary works such as poetry and plays. I am curious as to whether or not they would accept me. But i've never even attempted a test.

In addition to that, I attend public readings held by the Spiritualist Society in order to gain an understanding of how the various forms of media function.

My memory is very clear of a battle I had with a skinhead in front of a red phone booth. There was a woman from East Asia inside, and she was speaking as quickly as she could in a foreign language despite the fact that she only had a few coins with her. Even though I was the next person in line, the skinhead started banging on the door and screamed at the man in front of him to hurry up. I was the one who suggested that I give her space. When he realized I was of Irish descent, he yelled at me, "London phone booths are for London people!" I responded by stating, "Well, if they'd left us something of our own in our own countries, then we wouldn't need to use your phone booths with your hooker stickers everywhere, so shut the fuck up." There were three of his pals waiting in line with us, and if they hadn't started laughing at him because a girl had out-argued him, I think I would have smashed my face in. Praise be to God for protecting their dignity in the situation. When he was alone himself, he had to act as if he could see the humor in the situation. They all gave me a handshake as I ended my conversation, and then they backed up the driveway to let me through as if I were Bishop John mcquaid in Dublin, striding imperiously down Grafton Street during Christmastime.

A LESSON OR TWO

My relationship with Fachtna is quite close. He has a whole room devoted to bookcases that are stacked with vinyl albums. To my knowledge, no one else has as many records as he does. From the Dub Vendor in Ladbroke Grove, purchase all of the records that are currently featured on the Jamaican charts. He claims that he takes all of the floors with him whenever he moves them to a new location. It stands to reason that this is the reason why he does not have a wife or a girlfriend. Where was she going to store all of her things?

He has been giving me a lot of exposure to the new reggae tracks that were released in the past year. The one by Barrington Levy titled "Here I Come" about the guy who is forced to take the child by the mother of the child because the mother of the child does not want to be tied down is one of my favorites. The way that he employs his voice makes the situation tragic, yet at the same time it makes you want to leap for joy. He does not respond verbally when she indicates that she does not want the child. Simply shouting "Shuddly-waddlly-boop-diddly-diddly, w'oh, oh, oh!" is all that he does. And conveys the myriad of thoughts and emotions that a man might have in the span of a few seconds more eloquently than even Oscar Wilde could have done.

The music that Fachtna performs for me is really incredible, and I can't get enough of it. My sole previous exposure to reggae consisted of the songs "Israelites," "54-46," and "Uptown Top Ranking." But he tricked me with another man who went by the name Prince Buster. A tune with a catchy name called "Judge Dread." The judge is still handing down sentences of four hundred years to everyone in the courtroom, which has turned into a chaotic situation. And then there are the choruses, which are the catchiest yet most threatening of all, and they are backed by four trumpet notes repeated over and over with drums. And the bass and the keyboard were only playing chords without any accompaniment.

My visit with Fachtna's friend Leroy, better known as Lepke, began with him escorting me there. He is the proprietor of a pirate radio station known as the Dread Broadcasting Company (DBC), and he also operates a kiosk on Portobello Road where he sells reggae cds.

On weekends (Saturdays and Sundays), customers can shop in the Portobello market. It is a really popular tourist destination, and there are people there from what appears to be every nation on the planet. During the Saturday afternoons when customers wander about, Leroy blasts records from two enormous speakers that are located at the front of his stand. It is common practice in Jamaica to start a record over quite fast if it is deemed to be of high quality. Every time it goes off, the younger people walking by yell "Rueda!" at it. After that, they proceed on their walk. It's wonderful!

Next to the stall, on the sidewalk, Leroy has rigged up a microphone for people to use. When you buy a single that has vocals, you also get what is referred to as the "riddim" version of the song. This is a great move on the part of the Jamaicans, who release the backing track of the recordings without the vocals so that people can sing along with it. It's kind of like karaoke, except that Jamaican vocalists compose different words and vocal melodies on top of the same riddim, and all of the songs become massive hits.

On the very first day that I visited, Leroy entertained us with one or two riddims in the late afternoon. A number of young men with their hair braided down began to meander around the market from a variety of different directions, and they casually flipped through the stacks of records and T-shirts as they did so. They were nervously and enthusiastically curling their toes into the ground as they parked themselves in the region of their microphone. They were gazing from one side of the floor to the microphone and back again. However, it wasn't long until they could be seen inching their way toward the vicinity of their microphone. Lots of rocking back and forth, lots of biting of the lip, and lots of hand wringing.

It appeared like older men with the same type of braids were gathering as each young man took his turn at the microphone. These were men whose dances consisted merely of taking a step back and forth while occasionally raising a hand as if to warn others. An individual or object Leaning against the wall behind the stall, he attempted to listen to the young people singing, but he was unable to understand what they were saying because of their accents. Only four words had registered in his brain since they were yelled out at the top of their lungs each time they were mentioned in the song. They were known by the names burns, potato, Babylon, and blood. (I was also very certain that I had heard the word fire rhymed with the word liar.)

When I first noticed that the arms of all of the elderly guys would go up when those particular words were said, it piqued my curiosity. I was seeking for someone to chat to in the rear of the meeting, so I strolled around the side of the booth looking for them. The riddim remained the same, however the voices that were being heard through the microphone kept switching. A rotund elderly gentleman was seen leaning on his bicycle in the parking lot of a bar while lighting the very tip of a joint that he was holding with a pair of tongs. It was so long that it was wrapped around his head like a hat, yet it was still long enough to hang down the back of his blue shirt. His white hair was so long that it was wrapped around his head like a hat.

I moved my face so that it was in front of his, and I spoke over the music, asking, "Can I ask you something, please?"

He tucked the joint behind his back and asked, "What if I don't want hansa?" I said that?" I said that?"

He stated, "I may not want hansa."

I responded by asking, "What exactly are you talking about? I am not requesting that you dance at this time.

He advised him, "yuh ask, you may not want to hit Hansa."

It took a long time to get this concept.

I asked, "What is Babylon?" and the answer was "the river."

I confronted him by asking, "Why are you laughing?"

Once more, he laughed.

I questioned them by asking, "Why do they say 'burn Babylon'? And why do they scream that the Pope ought to be burned, and why do the elderly people dance in that manner, moving their fingers in the air?

She jerked her head back and began coughing and laughing at the same time. He questioned, "Where do you come from?"

I referred to it as "Ireland."

"Hmm," he murmured, and then he looked at me in silence for some seconds while his sunglasses were covering the bottom of his face. In the end, he said, "Hinglan himself?" and I replied, "I said that.""

"H-England owns h-Ireland?" you might ask.

I denied it," (We just do not have the time to get into that.)

"Well, give," he instructed, "nobody owns God too."

He stopped what he was doing for a second and looked at me.

What kind of things will you learn if you attend a church in Ireland? Will Dem demonstrate Revelayshaan to you?

Isn't that what I said?

He declared, "Those Catholics, the Pope, and everything else, none of them are Christian." That is why they did not arm you with any weapons. God will soon appear. The office of the Pope is the same as that of Satan, because the Pope himself is Satan. Daughter, have you recently purchased a Bible? Asked.

"Yes, I do still have some."

"All well, then, spend the rest of your life reading Prophet' an' Revelayshaan and listening to Rasta music. Babylon is known as the "courtyard of the devil." Because Revelayshaan insists that it must, it shall go up in flames.

After making this statement, he dismounted his bicycle and continued to Westbourne Grove when the sun was beginning to drop. After giving it some time to make sure he wasn't looking in his rearview mirror, I decided to follow him.

Todos los Santos was the name of the road that he dismounted on after taking a right turn into it. There was a betting shop, a record store, and a take-out business, all of which were located outside, where numerous other elderly men with lion hairdos and Jamaican accents stood.

I stopped my car in the entranceway of a building not far away from them and listened to the way they spoke. It was just stunning. This is an entirely new way for me to experience the English language. And they did not chat about sports or politics as other regular old men do; they did not discuss either. They sounded like priests when they spoke. The man with the long hair working in the record store was playing reggae songs at a very loud volume. The lyrics of the songs were full of Scripture, and the customers in the store were shouting and arguing vehemently about the verses as the light from the door shone on them.

I enter the record store and inquire of the older gentleman working there which book of the Bible each song that was being played comes from. I always have a notebook with me and use it whenever I go anywhere. After jotting down what it has to say to me, I head back home to read the passages. I believe that he thinks me to be humorous. He smiles at me so warmly that his entire face brightens up like a massive sun. He addresses her with the question, "What is today, little girl?"

The elderly always refer to me as their "little daughter" whenever we have a conversation together. They refer to me as their "little sister" whenever there are middle-aged guys present. They treat me with a lot of consideration. They are never allowed entry. They are highly guardian in nature. If I respond in the negative, they hand me some jerk patties. They are fine with my hanging around with them even if I don't say anything.

FLAMMABLE MATTER

I AM STILL GOING BACK TO LOOK AT PICTURES IN BOOKS THAT DEMONSTRATE HOW TO PLAY CHORDS. After attaching a capo to my guitar, I noticed that the chord progressions I am familiar with have shifted into different keys. I use the fewest feasible chords and don't get "fancy" with my playing. I am unable to form bar chords, and my playing is barely audible above a whisper. On my demos, the guitars are played twice. My recording setup consists of a four track machine, which is analogous to a tape recorder but also has inputs for a guitar and a microphone. In addition, I have a microphone stand that is bright red and a connected microphone that is black.

I own a Takamine twelve-string and a Takamine six-string guitar; both of these instruments have six strings. In addition to that, I possess an electric keyboard. As part of the arrangement that I had with Ensign, he was the one who footed the bill for all of this equipment as well as a variety of other accessories. Although I have everything set up in the sitting room of my home on Hither Green Lane, the recorder is portable enough for me to carry it with me everywhere I go.

While I quietly play guitar and record a recording, I sing the song's words to myself in my thoughts. After after, I play that back and record myself playing the other guitar gently next to it. After way, there are two guitars and it doesn't matter if I'm silent since there are two guitars. This kind of recording is helpful for me as well because layering the guitars allows me to conceal how poorly I play when I need to play loud. You can mix down a final tape for yourself by turning the levels of your guitars and vocals up and down during the song and drowning them out with reverb as you do so.

I bring the cassettes with me to Ensign and Chris and Nigel listen to them there while wearing headphones. They believe that I have a sufficient number of songs to form a band and begin practicing. After that, i'll be prepared to record whenever the appropriate time rolls around. They want me to become accustomed to singing my own songs and also want me to collaborate with other individuals on the creation of music. I'm relieved about that because it's one of my favorite things—especially given how poor my musical abilities are—to have someone else write the music.

Nigel gave me a piece of paper and told me to place it on the table at the Greek restaurant across the street from the Ensign office. He then stated, "Ali mcmordie of Stiff Little Fingers lives in Putney, and I want you to go there on Thursday morning at 10 o'clock." jaysus. I'm such a huge fan of Stiff Little Fingers that I almost passed out. "You are going to meet Ali, who plays bass, and a drummer buddy of his named John Reynolds. Ali's friend John Reynolds is a drummer. You are able to compose some songs with them."

On the day that they told me to go there, I went. I had to cross the street to get to the entrance on the right, and as I did so, I noticed a man who had just parked a black BMW and was now closing the door. He had ringlets in his hair and was dressed in a gray vest with green lettering that wrote MIKEY DREAD on it. He was equipped with two drumsticks. I asked him, "Are you John?" at the exact same time that he asked me, "Are you Sinéad?"

Ali's butt was cast in white plaster and displayed on the kitchen counter at his apartment. He invited John and I into the living room to hear some of the tunes I had written. They had a lot of praise for "Troy." They inquired as to the genre of music I was interested in composing in collaboration with them. I believe I just described myself as "not prim."

John and I ate our meals together in a restaurant during the lunch hour. During the course of our conversation, I started to get mental pictures of a bedroom.

As I indicated earlier, I often have mental images of the interior of other people's homes. This wasn't done on purpose. Just in the past. And there is no major, profound, or otherwise significant explanation for it.

Next to the bed is a table with a few trinkets or decorations on it. Curtains made of lavender fabric and lace, and a pile of letters stacked on a shelf. The curtains of darkness were pulled.

Because the visions were so vivid, I inquired of John whether or not he was familiar with the location. He said that it belonged to his sister Audrey and that she used it. And that she was in her final moments. I was overcome with grief. She was in a great deal of discomfort.

Even though he was taking care of her outside of London, he drove her into the city every day so that she could continue working. This allowed her to maintain her sanity.

John had a boyish appearance thanks to his well trimmed dark locks and his enormous blue eyes. However, he had the physique of a giant, and his hands looked like enormous shovels. Switching gears here. He started making sexually suggestive jokes. Using the word "c" more frequently than anyone else i've ever come across. I had the impression that our friendship would last a lifetime.

SHAVE MY HEAD

NIGEL IS A SQUARE ALL THE WAY TO HEAVEN, just like anyone else who shares his name, Nigel, is destined to be a square. A few days ago, both he and Chris extended an invitation to me to attend Ensign. I joined them for lunch at Khan's, and around halfway through, Nigel made the announcement that he would appreciate it if I would stop cutting my hair and begin dressed more like a woman. His disapproval of my latest effort at a Mohawk, albeit a very short one, was clear. He claimed that he and Chris would want her to wear short skirts with boots and possibly some feminine accessories like earrings, necklaces, bracelets, and other loud objects that one couldn't wear near a microphone. He also said that he and Chris would want her to dress in a manner that was appropriate for a young woman.

As soon as he finished speaking, I turned to Chris, who had been silently nodding his head in agreement with every word that Nigel had been saying, and I said, "So let me clear this up. Do you want me to resemble your lover and the woman he cheated on his wife with with the bird? There was complete silence as I stood up and rummaged through my pockets for my keys and cigarettes. Chris had a very handsome appearance. The enormous eyes that were fixed on him were unable to conceal their admiration for the observation or their wickedness at finding it to be so hilarious.

When I informed Fachtna about what had happened, he responded by saying, "I think you should shave your head." The following day, I made an appointment to get my hair cut. Greek restaurant is adjacent to a bathhouse close to the Ensign, and I was able to phone them immediately after the deed was completed. He had planned to stop by under the guise of having receipts to hand over to Doreen, his attractive secretary, who was a rather blonde middle-aged woman.

That day, the barbershop was run by a young man who was probably around twenty-six years old. I was in my nineteenth year at the time. In point of fact, he was Greek, with a five o'clock shadow, short black hair, and a tiny surplus of fat. It was clear that he had been left in charge alone, and despite the fact that he did not have any other customers save me, he was still in a difficult situation.

I climbed into the chair upholstered in red leather and declared, "I want to look like a boy." As soon as he grasped exactly what I wanted to say, which, because he didn't speak any Greek, I explained with a series of hand gestures that I believe may have initially confused him, he went to the phone that was hanging on the wall, possibly to she calls out to the owner, tears begin to fill up in her eyes. He didn't speak any Greek.

There was no response to this. It was only me by myself.

"I beg you, force me to do it! Please, he pleaded before hanging up the phone and walking toward me with his hands joined in prayer. His voice was as gentle as if he had been the one to deliver me himself, and he said, "Yourh beeeeyootheefil hayerh."

When she eventually walked across the room to face me, she could tell that I was not going to be persuaded, and when she saw the resolve in my eyes, she felt an unearthly horror well up inside of her, and she automatically put her hand to her neck to protect it.

He said with a very strong inhalation, "What does your father say?" and she asked as she let him out, "What does your bruddthar say?" After that, there was another short, quick gasp, followed by a frightened pause. After that, they said, "O maw Gowdth! What do you think your lover will say to you? Oh, the horror! When she heard this, her eyes shot out so far in response to her terror that I thought they were going to pop out of their sockets.

Because he didn't speak much Irish, he communicated with further hand gestures that he didn't want to risk any man coming to beat him up. He said this because he didn't speak much Irish. I reassured him that nobody would harm him, despite the fact that at this point I was contemplating hitting him myself.

After I had persuaded him that I was the sole author of my own destiny, despite the fact that I was a woman, and after I had conveyed that my father was in Ireland (I relayed it by dashing through the store with my arms outstretched like a plane and saying: " Irish! "), I was able to persuade him that I was the sole author of my own destiny. Daddy is in Ireland! "), she convinced him to go along with it. However, he never failed to make his feelings crystal apparent. "Gerril's life is a mess in every way."

After he had finished speaking, I rose up to face him, and I noticed that a tear was running down the right cheek.

Me? I was in love. It resembled an extraterrestrial being. It was very Star Trek-like in appearance. It was irrelevant at this point what he was donning.

Nigel's expression of startled quiet continued throughout the Ensign as I made my way through the room. Doreen, with her back turned to him, smiled playfully while giving me a thumbs up and a double thumbs up in silence. Chris invited me to ride with him later and spend some time in the car with him.

You asked why you left, and your response was, "Because I want to be me."

"Can't you just be yew with 'ayah?"

I responded by saying, "You are the one who needs hair, bald; not me." Why don't you let me assist you in locating a qualified medical professional?

THE LION AND THE COBRA

DEPENDING ON HOW LOUD YOU SING, THERE ARE SMALL LIGHTS BOTH ABOVE AND BELOW the enormous mixer. These lights can be red, yellow, or green. If you turn it up to a level where they become red, it indicates that the tape will be distorted if you continue to do so. The goal of my game has been to navigate the increasingly blurry boundaries between green and yellow in such a way that Mr. Happy, the game's producer, is forced to worry about his position fewer and fewer times.

Because I know I won't have much of a say in the mixes with regard to the level of the vocals, I need to make sure that every word and word ending that I sing in a whisper is heard. Otherwise, the producer will just get me down to whatever random level in the mix and leave me there. Words that were only heard in a whisper are gone forever, but I'm glad I wrote them down. Because of this, i've given my voice its very own master fader.

In order to accomplish this, I looked at the lights on my home recording equipment while singing into the microphone at a volume that was little higher than medium. I committed the location of the end of the green to memory and allowed it to permeate my body in the same manner that notes do; consequently, avoiding the yellow is now a part of the songs.

Within the confines of a particular triangle energy field, you are able to maneuver a microphone. The dimensions of each field change according on the microphone being used. Because the area in which they are able to pick up your voice is so limited, we sometimes refer to some ones as requiring you to be "on top" of them. Others have a broader playing field, and you can shift your body in order to get what you want even if the lights don't turn green. You allow your body to make use of the field in a manner comparable to how an actor makes use of a stage. Where do we draw the line between being too close and being too far? You may get a sense of it through your face.

I've just about reached the halfway point in recording my debut album. Nigel chose the producer, who is a fucking fool and has absolutely no sense of humor, and he needs it, considering how embarrassing he's making my song seem, given how bad his beard is.

Every time the producer puts on a new track, not only have I lost my own sense of humor, but I also feel like my enthusiasm for life is ebbing away a little bit more. It's almost as if i've been smiling on the surface while literally crying on the inside. Because I don't want to make anyone's feelings worse than they already are.

John Reynolds and Fachtna are the only other individuals with whom I have had this conversation. Since John is the drummer for the band, he has spent the entirety of this time in the recording studio with the rest of us. Therefore, we have frequently discussed the possibility of escaping to the opposite side of Mars in the event that the record is released with our names on it.

At first, the producer labored for a considerable amount of time to achieve just the sound of the bass drum or just the sound of the top hat. This served as a good illustration of how the term anal-retentive may be employed in a musical context. Prior to making a recording of a note. Tssh, tssh, tssh for the rest of the day. Who acts in this manner? Because he either couldn't or wouldn't take musical shitt, he kept the band waiting for whole days before they could play, which meant that I had to wait until late at night to sing. All of this was because he wouldn't or couldn't accept musical shitt.

He has a significant amount of gray in his wardrobe and almost always faces away from me while we are together. He occupies the producer's chair, which is always the largest of the three swivel chairs in the room, which is located in the exact middle of the soundboard. In point of fact, she does not so much sit as lean over the desk with her head in her hands. She does this rather than sit at the desk. A position that cannot be won. It would appear that he is making preparations to stage his own suicide.

A fortnight ago, Fachtna told me that even though I didn't know how to use the studio equipment, I could start again and make my album on my own if I wanted to. She stated this regardless of the fact that I didn't know how to operate the equipment. The only thing you needed to do was describe exactly what you wanted to an engineer. According to him, that was the only thing a producer did anyway.

"But," I questioned, "what about the one hundred thousand pounds that the record company has already spent on these recordings?" She couldn't continue to irritate Nigel in this manner or he would have a nervous breakdown. If I went through with it, it would be the same as if I had taken his one hundred thousand pounds and thrown them down the drain. Then Fachtna informed me of something that I was unaware of; namely, that the one hundred thousand pounds was my own money due to the fact that the contract stipulated that such charges were entirely recoverable. Nevertheless, I explained, I couldn't do anything to make Nigel feel bad.

But then someone asked me for something on Nigel's behalf, something that wasn't in our contract, and that was the moment when I stopped caring about his money or his feelings.

We were recording a rendition of "Crystal Ship" by The Doors on Friday night, and I was having trouble hitting a particularly high note in the song. That had never taken place in the past. After what seemed like a million and one futile attempts, I yelled into the microphone in a fit of rage. Neither of those things had ever occurred before. My first thought was that I might be pregnant when I heard it hit the ground. Before heading to the studio on Saturday morning, I stopped by the pharmacy and picked up a test. I had to urinate into a tiny glass tube that contained a small globule of jelly that was light yellow in color. After that, I had to set the tube on a small stand that had a small mirror underneath it, and a lovely pink circle began to form in the mirror almost immediately. It was also really gorgeous, appearing almost like a miniature planet.

I quickly hurried and grabbed a cushion from one of the sofas in the lobby area of the studio, and then I ran back to the bathroom to tuck it into my sweater so that I could see what I would look like all fat with a kid; I turned from side to side in the mirrors and jumped up and down in excitement. That much joy.

I told John the next day at Hammersmith Market that he was the father, and he couldn't believe it when I told him. John was the father.

I couldn't help myself and ended up falling head over heels in love with him. I was unable to have sexual relations with him any longer. Because I didn't want to add fuel to the fire, I didn't explain why. So I told him that there must be something wrong with me in terms of my sexuality. I just couldn't get it right.

When I told Nigel, he gave me a friendly smile and advised me to consult with the Ensign house doctor so that I could get my prenatal treatment started. The following evening, I went.

The doctor told me that Nigel had already phoned him and requested that he, the doctor, would impress upon me the following, which he, the doctor, said to me in the following words: "Your record label has spent a hundred thousand pounds recording your album. You have a responsibility to them to abstain from having this baby. In addition to that, he told me that my unborn child would be at risk if I flew while I was pregnant. And in any case, if I wanted to be a musician, I shouldn't have children because a mother shouldn't abandon her child while she is on tour, and on the other hand, you can't have a child with you when you are performing.

I can't remember the last time I sobbed so much. Nigel has no problem showing off his one hundred grand. And the one who produced it. I'm beginning afresh from scratch.

CLOCKS AND WOKS

Despite the fact that my annual income is barely five thousand dollars, I am at least one hundred thousand dollars in debt. If this record does not pay me back that money and more because it is the second time that it has been recorded, then I will never be financially independent from individuals who have penises. In connection with this topic, I should also mention that I am approximately as pregnant as a person can be. My enthusiasm level is through the roof right now because the baby is turning over so wonderfully. When i've been recording vocals there, I really hope the weather has been nice. Some of the songs consist entirely of shouting and yelling at the top of their lungs.

The previous week, I was asked to leave an Italian restaurant in Charing Cross by the elderly woman who managed the establishment because I was wearing a white T-shirt with the words "ALWAYS USE A CONDOM" printed on it. The shirt was cut so that my belly was exposed. She did not perceive the humorous aspect of the situation.

In Putney, I'm staying at an older establishment that serves as a bed and breakfast. During the time that we are mixing the album, I will be residing there for the next three weeks. There is only one flight of steps in this red brick family home, which is a tremendous blessing. The street appears to be one that one is familiar with. The homes have an appearance of coziness and warmth. On each of my nightstands are triangular handkerchiefs made of cream-colored linen that have dainty lilies stitched in each of the four corners. On the shelf next to the television is a glass jug with a belly similar to mine. The jug is filled with water, but its hope is in vain. I have not even come close to it.

Over the past few days, i've had a lot of fun making my way from the street to the studio by sauntering through the white fences and the overgrown trees. Overall, it's a significant step up from the Kypriana Hotel, which was our home base throughout our recording sessions. It is fittingly nicknamed a "kip" because that is what people in Dublin call a disgusting garbage dump in the local slang.

It turned out that there were fleas. In the middle of the night, John Reynolds and I had to put up with a variety of them and their sharp teeth. However, we did it willingly since we were well aware that being there meant that by some miracle we had become ex-thieves and that we now had the option to earn a living in a lawful manner. This made us very happy. If we hadn't been in the music business, the two of us would probably be breaking the law frequently and winding up in different prisons.

When John and I first met, the trunk of his car was stuffed with clocks and woks of all shapes and sizes. Because they were desperate for money and Christmas was almost around the corner, he and his accomplice had broken into a large warehouse. They intended to give some of the stolen watches and woks as Christmas presents to the women in their lives, while selling some of the items that they had stolen. John's mother went out and purchased a watch as well as a wok. The less revered girls were given any of these two options.

Meeting John Keogh is the aspect of the creation of our record that will stick out in my mind the most. Because he had just consumed a large amount of cake, he was currently lying on the ground outside the studio restroom and giving himself a bear hug. He stumbled through the greeting in his East London accent, "'Ullo, Shine-eyed," and then laughed to himself as his eyes rolled back in the sockets at the back of his head. I was about to step over him when he exclaimed, "Daan' warry, wow' look ap y' skuh." Just at that moment, I lifted my foot.
Max's bass player, he joined us while we were recording his song "Just Call Me Joe."
He has eyelashes that resemble the legs of a spider and they are lengthy and thick. His eyes have a very little greenish yellow hue to them. They remind me of clocks made out of dandelions. Because he's usually high on class A drugs, his eyes always roll up into the back of his head whenever he comes to visit me at my home, just like the snake in The Jungle Book. However, he is not a sly individual; rather, he is a straightforward Because of this, he can't take the outside world.

He is currently propped up against my door. He claims that he does not have any sisters, which is why he enjoys chatting with me. He appears to be amazed, as though he were a young child. He glances at me. I inquired after the reason. He stated that neither he nor I should have been asked to take on the responsibilities of an adult; rather, we should have remained children the entire time. He is astounded by the fact that anyone desires to become an adult.

Because she has a sort of teary-laughing chuckle, her grin makes other people smile. Because of the harassment he endures in his community, he makes an effort to conceal the fact that he is really attractive. He will either look away or gaze down at his hands. He dresses in a slovenly manner and has acne, and the color of his teeth varies from yellow to gray depending on what he eats. However, he does smile even after the hit has caused him to close his eyes. He possesses a high level of intellect. It is never for your own profit; rather, it is always for the good of other people. He would like for us not to be concerned about him. He would like it if we believed that he is fine. However, he is not in good health. In the end, he finds himself dozing off in the restroom.

Only the engineer, myself, and the person in charge of the tape operations worked on the mix. Most of the time, they are given the least desirable tasks. Having to get there earlier than everyone else and stay later than everybody else, while also having to run about and make countless cups of tea and coffee for the artists and producers. Having to leave the contingent in order to go to the store and buy sandwiches or satisfy any other desire the group may have. They are nerds, but only in the sense that someone like Superman would be considered a nerd. And while i've been observing them, i've come to the conclusion that there would be no records to speak of if it weren't for the nerds. There would be a large number of stoned musicians as well as stoned record executives. The latter would be too busy pleading not guilty to aggravated sexual harassment for being too high and getting away with it to be of any service in the recording process. There would be a large number of stoned musicians and record executives.

There is no other category of man who is qualified to carry out the job that gives rise to the term "tape operation." This man is capable of accomplishing something that no other man would have the guts to try. Because he has the least to lose out of everyone involved in the study predicament, his superiors are forcing him to participate in the study. But the fact that he is capable of doing it makes him superior to everyone else.

To create an edit on the tape, you will need to splice it.

If the first half of the song went well but the second half sucked, and it went backwards on the previous take, you can execute a Wilkinson Sword razor cut on the tape immediately before it all goes wrong. This will allow you to start over with the first half of the song that went well. Make a cut in the old tape just before everything went properly, then use a special adhesive to stick the two halves back together. This will ensure that the entire song is played correctly, saving you the trouble of recording everything over again.

In order to accomplish this, it first has the producer play the track, and then, once the desired edit point has been determined, it plays the track in slow motion around that place. The tape operator keeps an eye on the tape as it winds its way around the two reels while these plays are taking place. At some point, you will have to carefully grip the sides of both reels and spin them back and forth until the song slows down to the point when it sounds like a horror movie, and the voice will be very low. You are going to turn the cassettes over and over again until you locate the briefest pause in the music and make a note of where it is on the tape. Only after his eye can recognize it will he remove his hands, and at that time he will pull a four-inch stretch of tape from between the two spools onto a small steel bridge that looks like a leprechaun's train tracks, and then he will make a vertical line with tailor's chalk.

He has a piece to get back on track with. If you botch it, it will be a catastrophe for everyone involved. There is a significant amount of money in the room, in addition to a significant amount of artistic temperament. The knuckles are being held between the teeth with all of their might. During the one minute and fifteen seconds that it takes to make the cut, apply the glue, and play the tape, absolutely no one utters a single sound. Because he is the master of everything, there are never any problems; everything works perfectly the first time. He kicks his feet up on the cream-colored leather bean bag and takes a break from working as his superiors bring him a fresh cup of coffee and some biscuits. He is famous among celebrities for his work as a plastic surgeon.

MY BOY LOLLIPOP, JULY 1987

JAKE become BLU in his small blanket from head to toe in my room all over me, so I grabbed the nurse, and she grabbed him and went down the hall; she wouldn't allow me come with them. Jake had become blue from head to toe in his blanket. I was going crazy. An older nurse was walking by my door as I looked out the window behind her to see the opposite wing of the hospital, which was the section of the building where patients were taken to pass away. I grabbed her elbow and pleaded with her, saying, "My baby turned blue and they took him away, he's not going to die, is he?"

She responded with "I hope not," and continued walking.

Jaysus. Something like that would never occur in Ireland. You would find someone taking your hand. On the other hand, I am currently staying at the John Radcliffe Hospital in Oxford. I would say that I am twenty years old. This is my first child in any capacity. I have never in my life been so terrified of anything.

During the night that he was born, I had a horrible dream in which the doctor came into the room with the child wrapped in a blanket and brought the child to me. However, as I put the child on my shoulder, he tumbled off the bed. I woke up in a panic. Blanket and to the ground, and her little forehead shattered into a million pieces like a teacup. I really hoped that didn't portend a negative future for my abilities as a parent.

Praise be to God, he has returned. They kept him warm for one hour by placing him in an incubator. It is quite early, and she barely weighs six pounds and six ounces at this point. Because I am on the little side, so is he. The nurse reportedly stated such to be the case.

In addition to that, after it was taken out, I believe it was exposed to the air for an excessive amount of time. Because they were so preoccupied with the afterbirth, he became ice cold. It comes to sense that the outside of a body would be extremely cold given that it is warm on the inside. I had read nothing that should have alerted me, so I went without a blanket. In addition, there was not one in the delivery room. After what seemed like an eternity, he was finally wrapped.

As soon as I started having contractions, a friend of John's recommended that I consume a lot of castor oil. I'm not sure why I decided to take your recommendation. He indicated that it would simplify the delivery process. On the other hand, she is the one who informed me nine months earlier that day fourteen of a woman's cycle is the single day on which a woman is unable to become pregnant. He never mentioned to me that if I drank castor oil, I would have to urinate everywhere in Ireland, and the delivery would be so quick that there wouldn't be any time left over for drugs.

That evening, a low-income nursing student wearing a blue uniform was present. It is impossible for him to be older than eighteen years old. It was already far too late. She was obligated to keep handing me bowls made of gray papier-mache to defecate in, and then she was had to remove the bowls after they were full. I would guess that I filled perhaps twenty of them. The filthiest s*** i've ever seen, second only to what my sweet newborn baby did thirty minutes after he was brought into the world. That was like to toothpaste made of tar. As a result, I have to say that up to this point, I am really impressed with it. But also because it is incredibly adorable, fuzzy, and red in color. It resembles a baby monkey in every respect.

Jake entered the world at exactly four minutes and forty seconds in the morning. A long and trying night. After washing the blood off of me around five in the morning, John returned home for a little sleep. This was a chore that was generously handed to him by the midwife as if it were the highest honor that one could bestow on a guy who has spent the night seeing his pregnant girlfriend give birth. Your wife will give birth in and all over your nice white dinner shirt (a word of advice: never lend a full-term pregnant woman an item of clothing that you want returned). Your wife will deliver in and all over your shirt.

He's I'm not really satisfied with how it turned out. I had given it to him the night before, so in order to keep himself entertained, he decided to splash the tiles with cold water rather than lukewarm water. My response is that he asked me to do it, and anyone who puts someone with my haircut in charge of theirs deserves what they get. My argument is that no one would put someone with my haircut in charge of their hair. I managed to mess up the sides quite badly, and I have no idea how to mix. When he saw it, he was on the verge of tears.

However, I believe I have made amends because she adores her child and has given me permission to sleep in her blue and white nightgown. In addition, his mother is going to visit her first grandchild the day after tomorrow, all the way from Liverpool. The attractive woman who is John's mother. She has my love. She was born in Yorkshire and has the attitude of a preteen girl to this day. Consuming sweets when suffering from diabetes. She goes by the name Betty. Because she has such large brown eyes like Betty Boop, it works incredibly well with her.

Despite the fact that he owns a wild dog. There is no way that I will take Jake back with me. The number of postmen leaving their jobs continues. He converted his garage into a lovely front area complete with flower arrangements. A substantial window has been installed in place of the old garage door. The stupid dog always rushes through it whenever someone enters the house through the door. It is a Doberman pinscher. I despise it. The instant I encountered Betty, I was pushed up against the wall for a considerable amount of time. Humiliatingly awkward

John receives a lot of kindness from Betty. She is very smitten with him. She is only putting on an act when she reprimands him. When he is with her, he constantly farts loudly, which causes the two of them to laugh. The same might be said for Maria, John's sister. Betty is unaware that Maria has a large number of tattoos on her body.

I often wish that Betty was my mother. Alternatively, one of the children whom she brought up. She is really sweet and mild-mannered. His tone of voice is really comforting and friendly. The pitch goes up and down, just like a mother's voice should. Her children continue to pay her visits to this day. They have matured into men, just like John. They admire her, and she loved them even when they weren't following the rules and regulations. She is responsible for them having work. And then there are the girlfriends and everything else.

One of his sons lied to his fiancée about where he was going and said that he was going to get cigarettes around the corner. He didn't return for two years. After that, they tied the knot. It is enjoyable. He is going to be a wonderful parent to his children.

I want to make it perfectly clear that I do not blame John (or my dad, for that matter) for being concerned about the possibility of me becoming a mother. There were a lot of reasons to be worried about it. And I am aware that they only had the highest regard for me.

On the other hand, I do not believe this to be the case with regard to the record corporation. The only thing he seemed concerned about was money, in contrast to John and my dad, who were more concerned about my childhood. Concerns that are founded on love, to put it another way.

Because John is like a brother to me and my best friend in this world, he absolutely has the right to his own chapter in this book. Since I was eighteen years old and he was twenty-eight, we have been friends ever since. And that is a significant amount of time. Even when I was in the wrong, he was there for me as a friend and supported me no matter what. It has always been the foundation of my life. And he has never stopped looking out for my best interests.

When I was with John, I experienced some of the funniest experiences of my life, and I don't think i've ever laughed so hard with any other person. He did not fart out loud all that frequently either. John is renowned for his extremely loud farting. Additionally, it is infectious.

Today, his workshop is located on the second floor of the home that he shares with his incredible wife, Fiona, and their two children, Jesse and Ruby.

There have been many different kinds of artists that have worked and resided there. From Seun Kuti to Robert Plant, myself and Damien Dempsey, the Indigo Girls, and virtually everybody else you can think of. Because John is an outstanding maestro in the musical delivery room. He has the ability to make people feel so at ease (sometimes by farting loudly), and as a result, they are able to be absolutely authentic in a manner in which they would not be able to be in any other studio. He is able to bring out the very best in each artist he works with.

John is devoted to his two bullmastiffs, and he treats them as if they were his own children. Both he and Fiona are fantastic examples of what it means to be a parent. Within the confines of his home, I never once heard a loud voice that was not singing.

Jake is fortunate to have such a wonderful father in both his past and present lives. Jake, as they say in Ireland, is the "spit" for him, so thank goodness for that. They are practically identical.

I tried to find the words to express how much I care for John and how much his presence means to me, but I was unsuccessful. He is part of my family. And I wouldn't have sang virtually anything well if I hadn't been comfortable enough with him to be recording there in my pajamas and slippers, making me cry and laugh with farts emitted to the backing tracks... And if I hadn't been comfortable enough with him to be recording there in my pajamas and slippers, I wouldn't have sung almost anything well.

Without John in my life, I don't know where I'd be. Without the friendship, creativity, brotherhood, humor, and emotional support that you have provided me, I would be nothing. He is the rock upon which I build my existence. Simply put, there are no words. However, the body of work that we have produced together over the course of the past 35 years in terms of music speaks volumes and is the legacy of our connection. A graceful waltz across the years that we've spent together in this existence. To this day, I still have it. And I never will change my mind.

THE WAY YOUNG LOVERS DO

I GAVE JAKE HIS FIRST BATH WHILE JOHN WAS AT THE STATION PICKING UP BETTY WHEN HE LEFT FOR WORK. The poor animal let out a wailing howl; the sound was horrible. He was fuming with rage and his face was bright red. He is quite diminutive. Betty found her true love. She is wonderful. She presented him with a statue of a cute, chubby rabbit wearing yellow shorts and a green shirt, and smiling broadly.

Having Jake around was also a little unsettling at times. When John and I went out in the car one day, it was about a week after Jake was born, and we didn't know we had a kid until we were about a hundred feet down the road, we had forgotten that we had a baby. When we found out, I came dangerously close to having a heart attack. He yelled at the car and raced back to the house to get it.

Another night, I was terrorized by the thought that I had abandoned Jake with my mother, telling her she would have to take care of him while I went shopping. In all the years of my existence, I have never had such a terrifying dream. I woke up hot and immediately reached over to feel Jake in the dim light to make sure what I had heard wasn't accurate.

Babies typically do not smile at their parents for the first six weeks of their lives, and when Jakey does grin, it is the prettiest thing I have ever seen her do. His whole face as well as his eyes become bright. When he did it for the first time, he had been lying on his stomach on my bed.

My manager, Fachtna, was the only other person at that time who completely supported my goal of being a traveling artist while still caring for my daughter. John Reynolds was that person. He was the only one who believed that she could be a good mother and that she would make sure there was always help available. He said that she would make sure there was always help available. After two years of being his friend, he had become someone I looked up to as a role model.

It took three months for Jake to be born, and just as my album was ready to be released, the reviews started appearing in the media, and we started going on promotional travels.

I am twenty years old and I currently reside in the Blooms Hotel, which is located in Dublin. My arms and legs are trembling as I take a tray of coffee over to where Joe Jackson of Hot Press is seated at the bar waiting to interview me. He is interested in what I have to say. In order to promote "The Lion and the Cobra," our team traveled all the way from London. It's not me, whoever these folks I'm meeting with are meeting, and I have no idea who they are.

We are staying at the American Hotel in Amsterdam, and I am currently in a room where I am having conversations with ten different people on a daily basis. Each of these individuals has a microphone and a notebook in front of them as they listen. With cameras and white lights that flash constantly. Will I continue to be like way or will I change?

I have no idea what city or town we are now in. It makes no difference to me what we have for lunch. It doesn't matter to me why I broke the record. I have no idea what galaxy I'm now inhabiting.

Anything that Fachtna considers to be a good idea should absolutely be implemented. What he cherishes, I cherish as well. What he despises, I do my best to despise as well. My only goal is to maintain my standing as a formidable rival in his eyes. I utter everything I can think of that I think could impress him. I mold myself into what I think he will find impressive.

There are times when I feel like I'm more like him than I am.

THERE IS A LIGHT AND IT NEVER GOES OUT, 1987

I am currently on tour with inxs in the harsh cold of england. After i had already committed to going on tour with them, david bowie approached me about playing in his band. It was unfortunate that i would not be able to accept his offer, but i am grateful that he still asked me. My band include mike joyce and andy rourke, both of whom were in the smiths. Andy is the funniest guy i've ever had the pleasure of conversing with. It's wonderful!

When the parson came to have tea with andy and his brothers and their father, andy and his brothers would always be high. Around the table, the lads were instructed to maintain a composed demeanour and refrain from giggling and sobbing. One of the many reasons i like andy is that he is capable of both crying and laughing at the same time. Both crying and smiling at the same time is the best emotion there is, and it is the most enjoyable to see other people experience. He and mike have a great time when they are together. They both throw each other to the ground repeatedly. I share your passion for mike. They have instilled a deep-seated affection for manchester's locals inside me. Completely unambiguous. You're full of it. No less-than-honest discourse is permitted. In addition to this, they speak to me like i'm a kid, which makes this joyful girl more happier.

There isn't the same attitude towards women that prevails within music business groups (or that generally exists in ireland), and that mentality may be found among artists. Consequently, it feels great to be a lady when i'm on the road with the band and the tour staff. Because i spend most of my time with males, and because they treat me like a man, i'm gaining a lot of knowledge on how to behave like a guy.

If you have the confidence of a guy, becoming a travelling musician is a much safer profession for you. Not secure in the sense of being "safe from people," but safe from the knowledge that life on the road may be challenging and that you are an atypical lady in a state that is characterised as natural. You are behaving as though you are entitled to the same liberties as males. You're not going to be able to manage it very well. The house is traditionally the domain of a woman. That won't happen on highway 66. Particularly so if she's a mother like i am. If you don't constantly reminding yourself that you're a guy, you're going to spend the rest of your life racking your wits whenever you go to work. And this will continue for the rest of your life.

It is so wonderful when folks like andy or mike or john reynolds or john keogh or john maybury's group don't treat me any differently because of the fact that i am a female. Except when it's done in a good manner, like when maybury, the video director, hires someone to apply my makeup and constantly telling me that i'm gorgeous. It's about as straight as santa claus, which makes it even better than when a straight man says it, given that straight males only say things like that in an effort to get laid. It's something that john maybury and all of his other buddies say because they have a thing for women. They make me appreciate being a female in such a profound way. But i like having a masculine appearance. They have never batted an eye about it in any way. Nobody else does it. Aside from poor nigel grainge, of course.

I want to emulate john maybury's buddy alan as much as possible in my appearance. In addition to his dashing good looks and charming tenor, he sports a neatly cropped hairstyle. When she looks at almost anybody, her eyes are constantly sparkling with innocence and wonder. Always and everywhere, you can see his whole heart reflected in his eyes. He is not easily angered and has no fear of other people. I wish that i had his abilities. Since of my short fuse, i avoid most individuals since i am easily angered.

Not very long ago, maybury had successfully pulled off an incredible musical and advertising triumph. In spite of the fact that it is 1987 and there is an all-out conflict in northern ireland, maybury and his mad lighting guy were able to transfer kilogrammes and kilos of napalm from heathrow to dublin airport without being spotted at either end. They did this so that they could deploy the napalm in a film shoot. On a hill above dublin, we constructed the historic hellfire club, which dates back to the 18th century. It is impossible for him to have missed it five times. It has been designated as a national monument. Even asking for permission is not something that we do. The individual who was in charge of handling it was quite knowledgeable in the military. There was neither a fall nor a passage. We did not alter the framework in any way.

It was for the music video for my first track, which was titled "troy." the first half of the video was filmed in a freezing studio in east london. John enlisted the assistance of all of his close pals for the video project. I finally made it through to the other side that is unseen at either end, with the purpose of use it in a video shot. On a hill above dublin, we constructed the historic hellfire club, which dates back to the 18th century. It is impossible for him to have missed it five times. It has been designated as a national monument. Even asking for permission is not something that we do. The individual who was in charge of handling it was quite knowledgeable in the military. There was neither a fall nor a passage. We did not alter the framework in any way.

It was for the music video for my first track, which was titled "troy." the first half of the video was filmed in a freezing studio in east london. John enlisted the assistance of all of his close pals for the video project. I used a number of bics to give myself a clean shave and remove all of my head hair. After that, they coated me in pure gold leaf from my head to my breast, much like the girl in the james bond movie, and they set me down to sing in the middle of a circle of flames. John instructed me to continue "looking for the camera" as i was spending the day travelling around and around on a miniature railway track. My breath may set things ablaze, giving the impression that i am an angry extraterrestrial being.

In any case, let's go back to inxs. When we were all checking in at the dublin airport for the first tour date, that's when i first met michael hutchence. He treated me with a lot of kindness. He acts in much the same way as a big brother might. He looks out for others. There was no flirting or anything else. When i'm out with him, there are usually a lot of people around, but he always takes care of me in quiet, regardless of whether he's conversing with someone across the room on some couch or talking to pals or anything else. He's not around very often. He takes precautions to prevent any jerk from taking me to bed or killing me with endless conversation about the music business. He has my favour. The words don't really convey much of anything. He conveys the meaning with his glances. It reminds me of an american indian of some type.

During the tour, the bouncer of the nightclub that was located in the basement of our hotel assaulted andy rourke and myself in liverpool. Our injuries were quite minor. Huge creature with a lot of hair. It seems that he had served the british in belfast at some point. The moustache he wore, in addition to everything else, was really expressive.

My doc martens were not appealing to him in any way. That makes perfect sense to me. They feature steel toe caps that are projecting, and in keeping with the current trend, i have sliced the leather to expose them. And he did not like of the shaven head i had. Andy and i walked upstairs, and while we were up there, i changed my shoes. When we got back downstairs, though, i still had a shaved head, and we laughed about it.

At the box office, andy's face had an impish aspect to it. He couldn't control his uneasy laughter. Monster man came to the conclusion that we were causing problems and assaulted him. After that, he chased after us to the lift and assaulted both of us there. I was dragged out of the lift by one of his cronies, who grabbed hold of my shirt and pulled me out. Collar and up some steps, punching all the way, while monster man did the same to andy. Andy was also hit by monster man. They kicked us out into the street and left us there. We were both shattered to the core. I cannot find it. After that, we walked back down to our rooms, and once we were there, i hopped about for an hour while making threats to go down and murder him. Poor fachtna was forced to watch me sleep in order to prevent me from nodding off as she stacked chairs in front of the door to keep monster man out and me safe inside.

God chose to give the word "tour" a rhyme with the term "prostitution" for a very specific and meaningful purpose. In point of fact, the majority of what i recall about travelling was nothing more than sexual encounters, and this is particularly true of the time in my youth when i was doing major tours in the united states and europe to promote my records. That was the only thing that any of us had in mind. The concerts were performed by us. It was a pleasant diversion from performing the shows to do this instead. My bandmates and i, along with the other girls in our group, would often take the knight crew bus when we weren't too busy shattering hearts. Crazy, since in the united states of america you just do not do that, and especially not without your tour manager. On the roadways, each and every one of those buses was swaying back and forth.

On the other hand, i suppose that we ended up hurting several people's hearts when we decided not to continue our relationship since the majority of the squad was either married or had girlfriends at that point. It was very heartless of us to simply toss them out the window like a bundle of used tissues after the trip was over since we had become attached to them. Because we were just being whores, it was a ridiculous move on his part. As i already said, we thought they were really cool. They were great people, but as you probably are aware, they all had girlfriends, and in the music industry, we have a saying that going on tour doesn't count. That was the mentality that we had.

My second album, "i don't want what i don't have," was really supported by the tour that stands out most in my memory. At this point of time, he was represented by steve fargnoli, who had previously served as prince's manager. And due to the fact that the song "nothing compares 2 u" from the album had reached number one, i found myself in a whole new universe when i was on tour.

There was a production, complete with a variety of different forms of pomp and ceremony. There was a stylist. There were lighting people. It took me some time to get accustomed to it since i suffered from severe stage fright and had the overwhelming sensation that i was a complete and utter fraud. It was beyond my comprehension why my songs were well received, much alone why anybody applauded them or thought they were any good. When it came to singing or anything else, i really didn't have any self-esteem at all.

And there would be people screaming nearby on roller coasters, people screaming in panic, and i would be singing calming songs for the crowd while i was performing at these festivals or carnivals. It was the strangest and most upsetting thing that could have happened. I was also used to singing with my eyes closed, which was something that really irritated my management. I grew to like it for a variety of reasons, one of which being the fact that if you made eye contact with someone's partner, you were afraid that his girlfriend would strike you later, particularly if you were performing a love song at the time. I started to enjoy it because of this fact. In the midst of the shrieks of delight and the chilling anticipation of the wrath because of my envy, i was able to perfect the skill of closing my eyes while i was performing and transporting myself to another universe.

Spinning was, in the end, a very solitary activity. There were a lot of people in the room with me, including those that i really cared about, but no one could see me, and i could no longer see a reflection of myself in anybody else. All of a sudden, i was surrounded by people whom i had never seen before since i had become so renowned. I had cut myself off from my family completely. It is not your fault; the responsibility lies with me.

The touring experience, which consisted of me sitting in hotel rooms all day, was pretty isolating for me. And what exactly is the status of your promotion? Every time i spoke my mind, i got into some kind of problems. When people questioned me, i would answer their inquiries, and then he would be into problems. It was impossible to acknowledge him as a decent human being. It was painful to hear. Everyone started acting like i was insane as well, which made me feel worse.

You probably aren't aware of the truth that it does not make a difference whether you are the queen of england, barbra streisand, bob dylan, or anybody else; if you spit on a tour bus, you may be asked to leave the vehicle. On the door there will be a notice that states "no solid," so please don't bring any in. Because of this, the trip will be quite fascinating.

No solids would be the title of the "grooming book" that i would want to put together someday. I would love it if mariah carey, barbra streisand, and even the queen of england will share their life experiences with me by writing to me and sending me their tales. It would be a lot of fun if they were simply some extremely famous female celebrities, like celine dion, for example.

My own anecdotes of attempting to defecate aren't particularly entertaining. They are really a little unsettling, which is why i won't bother paying attention to them. I remember being lost in a field in france and being unable to see farther than a few feet in front of my face. I was on tour with sly and robbie at the time, and the bus was so near to me that i couldn't take a crap because i was humiliated. However, the bus didn't arrive, and the next thing you know, i was worried that everyone on the bus was going to get off, so i couldn't take a shit, and i was literally stranded there.

At some point, someone will get off the bus, which terrifies me to the point that i simply avoid looking at it altogether. When you're on a tour bus with fourteen other people, the fact that no one can crap on the bus means that you have to stop fourteen times, and at various hours of the day or night. I'm sure that other people have funnier tales than i have because of this. But i'm sure that other people do.

WHAT IS THE GOOD NEWS? WHAT IS THE BAD NEWS?

Within me, as fachtna said each word over the phone — "you've been nominated for a grammy" — i witnessed my life wrap up like a blanket and fade away as she told me the news. As swift as the speed of light, like a person who is nearing death. I have never revealed this to anybody. I've been told i resemble stevie nicks. She doesn't share her insights with anybody else.the nomination for lion and the cobra, which he received in 1989, was the turning point in his career. My second nomination, which came a couple of years later for the film i don't want what i don't have, offered me a great deal of happiness on a different level. Of course. This is due to the fact that nigel didn't take very long to phone and tell us that he didn't want us to release that record. To quote him directly: "it's too personal; it's like reading someone else's diaries." it will wind up collecting dust in a warehouse, much like the second record that terence trent d'arby ever released.i had been listening to the awful songs for a few months prior to the beginning of the recording process, and i had already mastered them. I was quite confused about what the heck i was doing. I guess he simply took pleasure in acting like a pig.i pointed out to him that my recording contract granted me full creative freedom, which meant that the album would be released regardless of whether or not he liked it.the guy is a perfect example of an oxymoron. How is it possible for a song to be too personal? I saw myself hitting him across the temples with a huge raw fish and giving him a gentle smack. Him's the only way to deal with idiots like him, unfortunately.i don't want what i don't have has become the most popular song in the whole globe in a couple of weeks, and nigel hasn't had to do much more than pick up the phone to make millions of dollars for himself. I am delighted for him. Because an idiot can never have sex if he is not filthy wealthy, and an idiot can never be filthy rich.my album's popularity may be traced back to its beginnings in a cemetery in paris, which was one of the aspects that led to its overall success. A bed in the size of a queen is sculpted out of marble that is snow-white in père lachaise. There is a young mother who is sleeping next to her infant while wearing an elegant buttoned nightgown and beaming at her child through the covers that are covering them both. The infant is also smiling. There is not a single imperfection to be found, right down to the tiniest creases in the sheets and blankets. Each and every crinkle that had been caused by the woman's smiling. Even her hair had made its way onto her pillow.i spent the better part of the day walking about in that location while wearing a very expensive coat that i secretly wanted i could retain. Père lachaise even had its own sewage system, according to gerry stafford, the stylist, who told me about it. I have to be honest and say that the concept of the dead rising to unoccupied spaces just to go back to their graves gave me a little bit of chills. In addition to that, how are they cleaned?reminder to oneself: under no circumstances should you ever visit a cemetery again.during that time, we were filming the music video for the song "nothing compares 2 u." a few days before, we had already filmed the majority of the video in london; there were maybe three sets total. In one of them, which was a close-up, i just sat in a chair and wore a black polo shirt while singing along with the music that was playing. But when it got to the line where it said, "all the flowers you planted in the backyard, mom, they all died when you left," i started crying and didn't stop for about twenty seconds.that probably indicates that i wasted their time. I was able to keep singing and arrange my show well. However, i believe that it is pointless. Therefore, it's to our advantage that we're filming everything in paris. Nevertheless, i feel terrible for wasting everyone's time and money in the process.john maybury, who directed my video once again, speculated that the reason i was sobbing was because fachtna and i had just ended our relationship. However, i am content with it at this point. It is beneficial to each and every person.   I was so upset by the loss of my mother that i started weeping. Despite the fact that i am now twenty-four years old, the event continues to cause me a great deal of distress. A little bit humiliating. However, there you have it. I myself am a female.

The areas of los angeles that are associated with the entertainment industry feature white walls decorated with gorgeous deep pink flowers. Some mexicans reside outside of mexico. The same may be said about african americans. The only time you see those folks is when they are cleaning someone's home. You never see them doing anything else.

In the new york headquarters of my record label, the mailroom is located in the basement, which has personnel with darker skin tones than the rest of the building. The higher up the floors they are, the lighter their skin becomes. In the same vein as the stations that the personnel have tuned their radios to. Two tales from up above, "no women" also turns onto the stage. Unless, of course, they are doing secretarial tasks.

Because the album cover shot for lion and the cobra wasn't to the bosses' liking, we had to come up with a new one for the american market that was still part of the same series. They had the impression that i was acting "angry" towards the european. It would seem that i am shouting. Actually, he was singing the whole time. The really astute photographer coaxed me into singing along with my record, which i had already cranked up to a very high volume. This is how i seem while i'm doing a musical number. However, my superiors favoured my "demure" appearance, which consisted of me looking at the ground with my lips tightly clenched. It would seem that ladies who give off an angry vibe do not "switch units." they are already suffering the consequences of my hair.

The folks who are in charge of the music business do not have any punk sensibilities. There are a lot of folks that are in fear. However, they are terrified of the wrong thing, namely music. As a result, the grammy awards included a category for rap music in 1991; however, the prize itself was not shown on television. Therefore, a boycott was organised among the rap community. As a result, i once shaved and dyed the public enemy insignia into the side of my head so that it would be seen on televisions in different parts of the globe.

Things started heating up in the entertainment industry. The young people are getting ready to riot, which hasn't happened since john lennon was murdered.

Rap is the most popular music genre in the united states. All you see are teens, who are referred to as "kids" by the adults in the institution, sitting on the stairs with enormous boom boxes and playing public enemy or krs-one at volumes so high that the bass practically makes you defecate, or dragging the boom boxes around the streets. On their backs, making it seem as if they were carrying out the stations of the cross.

The aim of rap, much like that of christ, is to boost the self-esteem of those who "previously considered themselves to be shit." therefore, it poses the same level of risk that christ's did. Because a large number of children of many backgrounds are listening, and no one in the business wants the top floors of their buildings to be endangered by someone with the incorrect thinking or the incorrect skin color—that is, someone who is concerned about the truth.children are the market, but you have to convince them that they are not as valuable as the stars; otherwise, they would not believe that they need the products that the stars are selling to them.hold off till you get to see. When the executives of the entertainment industry see that they cannot eradicate rap, they will kidnap it. They are going to turn pretend rappers become billionaires by having them say stuff like "you can't be like me."

Hilarious to watch how time passes by

When I was nominated for the Grammy Award for Best Female Rock Voice in 1989, I really went to the awards presentation in Los Angeles and sang the song "Mandinka."

Because the day before, when we arrived in Los Angeles, I had went into one of those small buildings on Sunset Boulevard that has a flashing sign in the window that reads PSYCHIC, I was apprehensive the whole time we were running through the dress rehearsal. I was worried because of this.

A middle-aged Indian lady with a round face and a fat figure came from behind a crimson drape while wearing a sari with orange and purple patterns. "Take a seat," he instructed me, indicating a worn out chair in a light green colour that was located to his left. After being absent for a little while, he returned and sat down in front of me while smoking his cigarette on the match.

We spoke for almost five minutes total. There was nothing in particular that came up, other than the fact that I informed him that my mother had passed away and that I was concerned about her wellbeing wherever she may be. She reprimanded me by stating, "That is not what I do. You are going to need a medium.

Then she said, "Let me see your palm," and I handed her my right hand. "Let me see your palm," she replied. "I see dark spirits around you," she remarked. "I see them all around you."

I'll buy you a big one. Why are they at that spot? How am I supposed to get rid of them?

She told me, "They are there because you are sad," and I believe her. After you get out of the shower, you should put some water in a bottle made of plastic and give yourself a bath.

He proceeded by saying, "You are required to secure a one hundred dollar bill to the bottle using elastic and then hand it over to me for each of your years spent on this planet." That will fix the problem.

ROSES MADE OF PAPER

MY SECOND NOMINATIONS FOR THE GRAMMYS CAME IN THE YEAR 1991. Because I wasn't there, the experience was extremely different than when I first received the honour. And I was given the prize for Best Alternative Music Performance, which I declined to accept. I know I let a lot of people down when I declined every award that was presented to me for my second record when they gave it to me personally. Because given the way he had spent the year being treated by the business and the media, he was aware that he was not going to earn accolades for anything that he stood for, so he did not bother standing for anything. Rather, I was receiving prizes because I had "sold a lot of records" and "changed a lot of drives." The level of commercial success was more important than artistic excellence. I was able to make a lot of money for a lot of guys who really couldn't have cared less about the subject matter of the songs that I was singing. In point of fact, I'd prefer it if you didn't tell anybody else about it.

I want to draw awareness to the issue of child abuse, therefore I have made it plain that I will not be accepting any prizes or participating in any award programmes. And that I'm not a pop star but a punk instead. And such prizes leave some individuals with a sense of superiority while others have a sense of inferiority. And the making of music shouldn't be a contest of any kind.

There is widespread indignation directed in my direction across the business. Jonathan King, a highly well-known TV DJ in England, is in charge of hosting the Brit Awards every year. For some inexplicable reason, he lashes out at me for my posture for the better part of 10 minutes. It's rather unsettling to think about. Because he is so upset, both of his eyes are swollen and he has froth coming out of his lips. How can the young Irish rebel say that music is associated with the abuse of children!

(His rage becomes understandable not too many years later, when he is found guilty of serial paedophilia and sentenced to prison for his crimes.)

When I'm in the United States, some males may be really intimidating, which is why I decided to avoid the Grammy Awards that night. In point of fact, I'm being bothered by it. At Eddie Murphy's place, where they were having a viewing party.Which terrifies the very daylights out of me.

After staying in Los Angeles for another three days, I fly back to England. I have decided to donate the house in Los Angeles that I own to the Red Cross. I don't want anything more to do with the symbols that are meant

SHEVITI ADONAI L'NEGDI TAMID (IN HEBREW:)

I attempted to enrol in classes that would teach me Jewish approaches of interpreting the Scriptures, but no one would have me as a student since I am not Jewish. I also haven't found the (much-fantasized) good-looking rabbi who is interested in marrying me and insists that I convert to Judaism since my love for him compels me to do so. Kabbalah studies with a wonderful instructor by the name of z'ev Ben Shimon Halevi at a little school located in the beautiful Regent's Park have been the closest i've been able to come.

After learning that "Nothing Compares 2 U" and "I Don't Want What I Haven't Got" had reached number one, it just so happened that I was enrolled in a class where the instructor and I were both aware, with regret, that it would be our last time together in a few short days. In North America. When I found out, I was sitting on a toilet (can't recall whose) with the door open as usual (for ease of communication), thus it was only fitting that I should be in that same position. Whoever told me that was angry with me because I did not respond positively to the news that they gave me. Instead, I sobbed like a baby at the entrance to the underworld.

In my dream that night, I was a golden orchestra triangle with limbs, legs, and a face, and I was travelling through dusty ancient alleyways in Regent's Park. People were fleeing the scene while stealing various parts of my body. I had no choice except to dash back to my house, change into an old raincoat, and conceal myself everywhere I went. If people knew that I am made of gold, I would be completely consumed by the public one day, and nothing would be left of me.

As soon as I arrived at my last Kabbalah session, the instructor pulled me out of the entrance of the classroom by my elbow, brought me into the corridor, and shouted in my ear, "Do you know that celebrity is a curse? When the adversary is a chivalrous knight?"

After I gave him an affirmative response, he led me back inside and said, "Don't forget to leave the party before everyone gets drunk and starts fighting." I nodded in agreement.

After a tour that lasted nine months, it finally came to an end, but my management wouldn't let me return home until after the MTV Video Music Awards, so I leased a house in Los Angeles instead. House with a Spanish appearance located halfway up a hill. The façade was finished in a stunning vintage white stucco. Even a little cross affixed at the front door, as is customary in Ireland. When I am standing in my yard, I can look to my left and see the Hollywood sign. There are moments when I look to my right and see a deer meandering among the woods.

The whole wall of the downstairs living room that faces Los Angeles is made up of windows made of glass. During the night, it resembles a pitch-black border surrounding the blazing lights of living hell. My nerves start to fray every time it's getting dark outside.

I choose to use a purple paint for my bedroom. My first impression was, "What the hell, you can have a purple bedroom in the United States; that's the point." Unless you were a prostitute, no one in Ireland would ever have a bedroom decorated in purple. And since having sexual relations is considered a sin in Ireland, it is impossible to work as a prostitute there because there is no market for your services. It seems that Archbishop John Charles mcquaid is the only person who has ever had a bedroom decorated in purple.

The phone rings in my bedroom on a weekday morning just as I'm trying to decide what to dress for the day. A feminine but agitated male voice says, "That Shine-head O'Kahn-er?"

I tell him, "No, this is Sinéad O'Connor," simply to get under his skin and make him angry. So I question him about his identity.

He claims to be the Crown Prince.

He has informed me that he plans to bring me a vehicle at a later time, and we are going to hang out together.

When Lion and the Cobra came out, I met him in a club, but we never really spoke to one other after that. We began with the music that the DJ was playing, which included songs by Sly Stone and other artists.

Since then, we haven't exchanged any words. It has absolutely nothing to do with the recording that I did of "Nothing Compares 2 U." Your phone call to my purple room marks the first time we've had any kind of communication with one another since the year 1988.

I have reached the age of twenty-three. When I tell my friends that Prince called, they immediately start daydreaming about being in a romantic relationship. Everyone speculated that he and I may eventually develop romantic feelings for one another.

Because the delightful Steve Fargnoli, who later became my manager, had handled it in the past and introduced us, we thought that at the very least he and I would get along well.

We reasoned that he must have been trying to honour the song by performing it to such a high standard. There will be cake at this event! There is always cake for the princes!

When I finally informed my unfortunate pals what had occurred, they were shocked since I had gotten it incorrect three times.

At nine o'clock at night, I see the long black limousine come to a quiet halt at my door from the obscurity of the bedroom window in which I am positioned. I like to believe that I'm in a movie about spies and that I'm going to be taken to a top-secret location where i'll be given my next mission.

Behind the wheel sits the archetypal driver, dressed in a suit and wearing a hat. Since I'm a chatterbox, I make sure to ask him everything about Prince and how the home is doing and other related topics while we're driving. He never speaks a word, but he sometimes gives me a terrified look in the rearview mirror, as if I had asked him how to travel to the castle of Dracula. Certainly peculiar. In most cases, male drivers like chitchat just as much as female passengers.

We go for a considerable distance before twisting up a pitch-black hill, at the crest of which stands a large home that is just barely illuminated. We pull up in his driveway and halt here. To my right is the entrance to the lobby. It seems like we are in a courtyard, and I can make out several rooms beyond the courtyard, perhaps sixty metres in front of me. This is about where we are.

I exit the vehicle, and the driver indicates with a nod that it is okay for me to go ring the bell by myself. This I have done. I wait for a few seconds, but nothing seems to happen. I try calling one again, but to no avail. I decide to turn back and ask the driver for his advice on what I should do, but he along with the limo had already disappeared.

The door opens with a creaking sound just as I am coming to the realisation that I have no clue where I am or how to go home if no one is there and the driveway is so dark that I won't be able to see beyond my eyelashes to get there.

My first thought is that the person responsible would ask, "Did you call?" much like in the movies, where the bad guy is always named Igor. It has come to light that Igor is not even his real name. However, I don't become aware of it until much later.

It would seem that nobody speaks in this location; all you see are head motions. He instructs me to go inside and then proceed to follow him. In doing so, I see that his demeanour has a certain air of "Master, Master," even if he is not nearly dragging a leg at this point. She is attempting to shield her heart by lowering her chin, keeping her arms at her sides in a straight position, and shrugging her shoulders.

We make our way through two enormous reception rooms that are completely dark with the exception of the weak light that seeps in from the hallways. In each, there is a window that is entirely covered with numerous layers of aluminium foil that have been coated quite thinly. I would estimate that the window is twenty feet high and ten feet broad.

"What's the deal with that?" I smile at Igor as he checks behind him to make sure there is nothing in the darkness that I may trip over. When I see him for the second time that night, he says those four words, which are the only ones I hear him speak the whole night: "He doesn't like the light."

When I see him a second time, his whole self, including his body, is frozen with terror.

But for the time being, I am brought into a tiny kitchen that is surprisingly brightly lighted. In the centre of the room is a square breakfast bar that is modest enough that people could sit around it if there were stools. Igor, poor Igor, is disappearing.

After a sufficient amount of time has passed without anybody approaching, I decide it is safe to swiftly investigate the cabinet located below the sink in order to find out the cleaning supplies Prince employs. After all, there isn't a single lady on the planet who wouldn't like her home's kitchen to shine like a castle.

I quickly realised that things needed to be cleaned up in there, so I got to work on that for him. Soon, I will hear a swooshing sound, and I will smell something delicious coming from someplace behind me. I complete the turn. There is a Prince at the door. Padded wrist cuffs Prepared to be fed to the canine.

It seems as if he is covering his face with virtually every bit of makeup that has ever been put on Boy George's face. It seems that I did when I accompanied Jerome Kearns to the prom when I was in high school.

"You must be Shine-aid," he says to me.

"You must be Prance," is the response that I provide.

There is a breakfast bar in the middle of us. He stays on this side of it. You'll find the refrigerator to your right, and i'll find it on my left. "Do you want something to drink?" He shows a grin.

"Yes, i'll take anything that doesn't contain alcohol, please." In light of this information, I do not like drinking alcohol since it causes me to hurl up, and Cinderella should never appear like she is throwing up. This is likewise the case; my grandma instilled in me the importance of being polite and expressing gratitude at all times.

As he searches the cabinet behind him for a drink, he turns his back on you. Then, in what seemed like the blink of an eye, he turned around, struck the glass in front of me so hard that I don't know how his palm didn't go through it, and said, "Get it yourself."

This isn't the first time i've seen it. It was always a part of my life. It's like second nature to me at this point. Without taking my eyes off of him, I begin to mentally scan the area for possible escapes.

It has now occurred to me that I have no idea where I am. I never inquired about the person's address. I am unable to locate the entrance to the building. It is nighttime. I have no idea where to start looking for a cab. I have no idea where I am other than that I'm up in the hills and far away from the road. In addition, it does not seem that you brought me here to enjoy some cake.

He starts pacing up and down the breakfast bar with his arms crossed, one hand rubbing his chin between his thumb and forefinger as if he had a beard, and looking at me as if (a) I'm a piece of dog shit.. On the toe of his shoe, and (b) he's trying to figure out where on my little body to hit me for the greatest possible impact.

This is not to my liking. Which is something that I do not appreciate. To add insult to injury, I take exception at the presumption that I am a weakling. Because I am Irish. They were unique in their own way. Who you are is completely irrelevant to us. We have been colonised by the worst of the worst in terms of spirituality, but we have emerged unscathed.

As a consequence of this, whenever he shouts at me and says, "I don't like the language you employ in your newspaper interviews," I respond by asking him, "You mean English? Oh. We're sorry, but the Irish were faster than us." "Does not say. "Your foul language makes me uncomfortable."

I tell him, "I don't work for you," and he seems surprised. "If you don't like it, you can just fuck yourself."

This really, really, really irritates him to no end. However, it suppresses it in a fury that cannot be heard.

As he exits the kitchen, I here him calling out many times to someone he believes to be called Duane. Every time he shouts, his voice travels farther away, so I know I have some time to hunt for a rear entrance. Unlucky. And in a little while, I will hear his footsteps, as well as those of Igor, coming back.

I don't even think they've made it to the door yet when I hear him calling my name. I have to go in the same direction with him for a little while till we reach a cosy dining room. This is something that I do, and as I go by Igor, I see that he has his eyes fixed on the ground and appears afraid, his body frozen in submission.

At the moment, I am seated here. I am now staring in the direction of the patio. He is standing directly to my left. He yells a harsh instruction at Igor as he descends the flight of stairs. He has a desire for soup. He asks if I would like any of it. Because I don't want to take part in mistreating Igor, I pretend that I'm not hungry in order to get out of it.

Where we are seated, there is an extremely insufficient amount of light. We are not making any statements at this time. Currently, he is meditating. He shouts once again, and after a while, poor Igor comes stumbling up the stairs holding a silver tray covered in linen of a cream-colored colour. On the tray, there are two bowls of soup and two spoons. He acts as if he is a beaten kid who is going to get another beating. His hands are trembling, and he is cowering before you like some kind of devil. It's the exact same crippling terror that my mother instilled in my younger brother on a regular basis. Igor gives off the impression that he is about to urinate on himself. In addition to this, he gives off the impression of being stoned.

He is seated at the table with his instructor in front of him. Does not bring the tray to the floor.Perhaps a minute and a half. He has his head bowed. It would seem that Oliver Twist is demanding more.

He tells himself, "You can quit now," the conversation is over. Igor acts in this manner. After that, he takes a few steps back while clasping his hands together like they are wearing a cap. I have a feeling that I already know what is going to take place.

He shouts at Igor, telling him to get Mrs. O'Connor some soup.

My response is "I don't want soup, thanks," which I say in a polite tone while rubbing my stomach and looking at Igor as if to say, "I'm sure it's delicious but I'm full" (this is something that my grandmother taught me). Igor's head is still stationary, but his eyes dart back and forth between me and himself before returning to the ground.

In the manner of Mrs. Doyle from the BBC series Father Ted, he proceeds to insist that Igor offer me some soup on many occasions. Only, in contrast to Mrs. Doyle, he talked in a tone that was so insulting and humiliating that it caused poor Igor to tremble even more, and he pleaded with his eyes for me to allow him to serve me the foolish soup. But whenever she got close enough to me with the bowl, she would stop, put her hands on her hips, and exclaim, "No thanks."

Igor was aware of everything that was occurring. I was not going to take part in embarrassing him in any way. Even if the fate of my life had hinged on it, I would not have consumed the soup. Finally, she placed the bowl back on the tray and stood there holding the batch, looking as if she were about to weep since she did not know what to do next.

Igor remained silent for a little while as he awaited the beginning of his spanking. It has here at last. It is then that he himself turns his wicked little face to my and says, in a tone that regular people would use when talking about faeces, "This, by the way, is my brother Duane."

I cannot believe it. And it makes me sick to my stomach that he was able to be so cruel to his brother. This is something I say just as poor Duane leaves the room. The temperature rises.

At some time, he comes to the conclusion that he and I both need to take a deep breath and calm down. He then heads upstairs, where he is most likely going to powder his nose and check to see whether the painting of Dorian Grey is still secure in the attic.

He sits back down on the couch with two pillows and suggests, "Why don't we have a pillow fight?" Everyone is kind and smiling. After the shaky beginning, I'm thinking, well, it's not every day that you get to have a pillow battle with Prince, so what the well, let's try to make the evening more enjoyable.

When I take my first hit, that's when I realise there's something in the cushion, tucked into the end, that's meant to harm me. Before that, I had no idea. He is not even pretending to play at all.

My temper flares up often. And also a great deal of fear. After trading a few more strikes with his opponent, he gets back up. At this point in time, we have navigated our way to the area just to the side of the main entrance. After opening it, I immediately leave. The chauffeur of the parked limo may be seen dozing off inside the vehicle. I really don't want to rouse him from his sleep. However, there is

The sun will have risen by the time I have completed going down for the night. I have a sense of relief. Silver shines from everywhere and illuminates everything. I rush on with my head down, desperately attempting to make it back to Los Feliz. Both the ride itself and the whole experience had a very similar feel to them. Easily may have been in the Glenagearyneighbourhood. In the meanwhile, I'm keeping an eye out to make sure that he isn't the one who pulls over to offer me a ride.

After that comes him. He follows closely behind me in his car, rolls down the passenger window, and barks orders at me as his left hand rests lazily on the back of his head. I inform her that she is free to suckle on my dick. Or anything along those lines.

He comes to a screeching halt in the slow lane and then exits the vehicle. As if he hadn't seen track one at ten at night, he begins pursuing me around the vehicle and warns me he's going to kick me.

I give chase to him, and we end up running around the vehicle for a few seconds together, with him becoming more frustrated that he is unable to catch me, and with me spitting on him like a cat that has just given birth.

Since i've lived out here for quite some time, there are now residences on both sides of the road, and most of them have driveways that are little more than six feet long. After informing me that he was a police officer, my father once advised me that if I was ever in a scenario with a guy that was similar to the one described above, I should seek assistance and try to ring someone's bell if it was feasible to do so. And i've decided to go ahead and do this.

First, I give the moron a chase for a sufficient amount of time to study his behaviour pattern. Because he needs to take a moment to glance to his right before dashing into the road, I can anticipate when I will be able to take a break. As soon as it happens, I immediately stop playing a record, go to the first bell on the record, and continue playing it.

He immediately gets back into his vehicle (my father was correct). He takes a seat and looks at me for a while, as if he's considering running a few more laps just in case I don't react to his question. However, he makes the decision not to take the risk. He is sensitive to the sun's rays. Someone could have been able to see it. Make the automobile go in the other direction and step on the gas. When he walks by me, he doesn't even bother to glance to my left.

I've been doing this for years, but no one ever answers when I call home. I am certain that it is no longer there.

When I reach the first phone booth, I immediately contact my roommate Ciara, who is also my best friend. I am going to be picked up by her. I have approximately a half an hour till I get home.

When Steve Fargnoli finds out, he completely loses his mind. He intends to revolve around and fire a shot at Fluffy Cuffs. In the same manner as one of his other Italian-American buddies. They allege that I have been the target of an assault that was really intended to make Steve feel terrified.

It would seem that he and Prince are now engaged in some kind of legal process. Other than that, I don't know too much about it. It doesn't matter to me either way since I never want to see that demon again.

However, I do think about Duane with affection pretty often.

The sun will have risen by the time I have completed going down for the night. I have a sense of relief. Silver shines from everywhere and illuminates everything. I rush on with my head down, desperately attempting to make it back to Los Feliz. Both the ride itself and the whole experience had a very similar feel to them. Easily may have been in the Glenagearyneighbourhood. In the meanwhile, I'm keeping an eye out to make sure that he isn't the one who pulls over to offer me a ride.

After that comes him. He follows closely behind me in his car, rolls down the passenger window, and barks orders at me as his left hand rests lazily on the back of his head. I inform her that she is free to suckle on my dick. Or anything along those lines.

He comes to a screeching halt in the slow lane and then exits the vehicle. As if he hadn't seen track one at ten at night, he begins pursuing me around the vehicle and warns me he's going to kick me.

I give chase to him, and we end up running around the vehicle for a few seconds together, with him becoming more frustrated that he is unable to catch me, and with me spitting on him like a cat that has just given birth.

Since i've lived out here for quite some time, there are now residences on both sides of the road, and most of them have driveways that are little more than six feet long. After informing me that he was a police officer, my father once advised me that if I was ever in a scenario with a guy that was similar to the one described above, I should seek assistance and try to ring someone's bell if it was feasible to do so. And i've decided to go ahead and do this.

First, I give the moron a chase for a sufficient amount of time to study his behaviour pattern. Because he needs to take a moment to glance to his right before dashing into the road, I can anticipate when I will be able to take a break. As soon as it happens, I immediately stop playing a record, go to the first bell on the record, and continue playing it.

He immediately gets back into his vehicle (my father was correct). He takes a seat and looks at me for a while, as if he's considering running a few more laps just in case I don't react to his question. However, he makes the decision not to take the risk. He is sensitive to the sun's rays. Someone could have been able to see it. Make the automobile go in the other direction and step on the gas. When he walks by me, he doesn't even bother to glance to my left.

I've been doing this for years, but no one ever answers when I call home. I am certain that it is no longer there.

When I reach the first phone booth, I immediately contact my roommate Ciara, who is also my best friend. I am going to be picked up by her. I have approximately a half an hour till I get home.

When Steve Fargnoli finds out, he completely loses his mind. He intends to revolve around and fire a shot at Fluffy Cuffs. In the same manner as one of his other Italian-American buddies. They allege that I have been the target of an assault that was really intended to make Steve feel terrified.

It would seem that he and Prince are now engaged in some kind of legal process. Other than that, I don't know too much about it. It doesn't matter to me either way since I never want to see that demon again.

However, I do think about Duane with affection pretty often.

THAT IS THE REASON WHY THERE IS CHOCOLATE AND VANILLA IN THE WORLD.

IN ADDITION TO BEING A FANTASTIC MUSIC MANAGER, Steve Fargnoli oversaw the operations of many establishments that can best be described as legal brothels. According to the legislation in England, a household might legally include both a working woman and a secretary. Both a "normal sex" room as well as a "hit me" room would be available. Steve was a professional pimp. He did not make use of the services that were offered by the ladies. However, they used him to their advantage. I mean, he provided financial support to these individuals, mostly due to the fact that he was fascinated with what he referred to as "the underworld" and attractive ladies who had tragic backstories. By the way, the music industry and the prostitute business are quite similar to one another. In point of fact, they are identical. On a Thursday, he gave me a call to tell me that he couldn't make it to a meeting that we had scheduled for the following day. "I just can't do it," he says to himself. "We are going to put you in a dungeon tomorrow night, the cross is coming." That is exactly what he did with the twenty percent he had. It was pleasant and enjoyable.

One of the females that was in his workplace on a Friday night during the holiday season was what I like to refer to as "the Christmas lady." A foul-mouthed blonde lady. A dominant woman who had a ferocious spirit and nearly had a deadly hatred for men. Even though Steve had been taking care of the office, some of his handlers, including Steve, nonetheless managed to steal from it several times. He was, in point of fact, an idiot. Genuinely good at heart Distracted by baby talk and boobs at the same time. There are really some men that are like that. (Or it once was.)

In any case, as I am beginning to question this woman about what she does and how everything works, she produces a letter that was written by one of her frequent clients. She tells me that males who want unusual things do not want it for sexual reasons; rather, it has nothing to do with sex; rather, they simply want to be treated like trash. She says that this has nothing to do with the fact that they want the weird stuff. She gets a kick out of being horrible to them. Neither for the reasons of his sexuality. Simply due to the fact that she is a complete whore.

In the letter, the man writes that he will be thinking about her throughout the holiday season and that he plans to work on his "barking techniques" while she is away. I don't care if you think I'm old-fashioned; I had to inquire as to what on earth he was referring about. She claims that he phones her every night at seven from his workplace, and that she makes him sound like a dog barking on the phone (my first thought is, what about the people who clean the office?). She claims that he has returned, and the agreement is that she will treat him like a dog. She is a huge fan of kicking it. She claims that she has him taste bowls full of his faeces in order to push him farther than he anticipated, and then she proceeds to humiliate him. Putting him through the motions of a dog crawling on his hands and knees. She is a bad person. The worst possible thing. So that she can put on this performance of being "the other lovely woman" when the males who engage in "normal sex" arrive there. The fact is that she would stab her own grandma if she had the chance. These unfortunate young men are clueless about their surroundings and have no idea who or what they are in the company of.

Steve has served as my manager for the better part of a dozen years now. After a Prince concert at Camden Palace, to which he had been invited for some reason, I was able to talk to him there. It had been a while since the release of my debut record, and it had been much longer since "Nothing Compares 2 U" had made its way into my head.

Newport, which is located in Rhode Island, is his place of birth. His father had a business of some kind. Sly Stone was able to go on tour because his father provided all he had to him in order for him to do so. And since Sly didn't go on tour, Steve's father ended up filing for bankruptcy. When Steve was a youngster, he travelled to Los Angeles and tried to locate his father. I was sneaky and managed to break down his door. He coerced him into leaving the house and going on the journey so that Steve's father could get the money. That's how Steve broke into the industry of making and selling music. In point of fact, prior to that, he was employed at the Newport Jazz Festival, where her duty was going up to Ella Fitzgerald's dressing room and announcing to her, "Five minutes, Miss Fitzgerald." He shared with me that he had been a vocalist in a band in the past, but that he quit after hearing Robert Plant sing. He said that there was no need in prolonging the conversation.

The next time I met Steve was at a picnic on Hampstead Heath with several of his friends, which was not long after the Prince event that took place at Camden Palace. Only for sake of social interaction. It was a bright and pleasant day. He was hilarious, the type of guy who would make you not want to go back to your house at all. When things became tense between Fachtna and I, I urged Steve to step in, and he did so with a great deal of enthusiasm.

It has the appearance of a teddy bear. He has white hair and big cheeks, and he is fat in the way that an Italian kid who enjoys food would be expected to be. He has to have his heavy spectacles on at all times since he cannot see a thing without them. Rose is the name of her young mother, and she used to have get-togethers at her home in Malibu for her circle of females, along with us, where she would prepare an endless array of delicacies. He treats her as carefully as if she were made of gold. She certainly is. He is completely enamoured with her.

His father has been gone for a very long time. Steve is like a dad to everyone. Except for his princess daughter, of course.

That's one of the things that causes tension between us, the fact that he didn't spend enough time with his kid.

Anyway, Steve is a huge fan of exclusive dance clubs as well as women in general. One night, the four of us went out with him and some of his friends to some clubs in Atlanta, where we ogled the breast job and one of his buddies, with whom I am head over heels in love. I can confirm for you that there is sexual activity taking on in the champagne room.

Steve is the one who has captured the heart of journalist and broadcaster Janet Street-Porter. However, they are the closest of friends. We can't help but feel a bit smitten with him. But he has no interest in having sex with anybody or going somewhere that offers it. He cannot get over the fact that the woman he loves is a very demanding German bird who works for MTV. However, she has a knack of consistently shattering his heart. The strategy of "reach and retreat" is executed by her with more skill than by any man. She had been making threats to marry the prominent Pakistani Imran Khan up until not so long ago. I was out and about while covered in a hijab. However, he has recently disappeared and wed Jemima Goldsmith. According to Steve, everything has turned into one huge drama, and he wants to be taken care of right now. When we go out and she is there, he consumes green alcohol, which puts him in a bad position. It's the equivalent of a child being in a candy shop.

The fact that Steve is rapidly expanding his wealth makes him a desirable target. Keep in mind that I was Prince's director at one point. In addition to that, he runs additional enterprises, all of which are trustworthy. He is the kind of guy who helps others. Every single girl with high standards is looking for a wealthy partner. The only obstacle is that if you get Steve, you get all of us as well, and you obviously have to get through Janet Street-Porter first. It is not a simple undertaking. Since she is affluent as well, and she loves him, they really complement one another and would make a wonderful couple. She does not desire him for the same reasons that other women of her social standing do not. Steve and she are able to get a giggle out of one other. She is in love. Except he has nothing except affection for ladies. This is how things stand with Steve. Not a suitable candidate for a boyfriend or spouse.

Aside from that, Steve is the person I admire the most. He is a divine being who descended from heaven. And I really hope that heaven does not want it. Because he suffered from cancer, his medical team insisted that he undergo a variety of ineffective and painful procedures around the city. He has wasted two years of his life going through unimaginable suffering for nothing.
People who work in the music industry often find that they can only really relax and feel at home in hotels. Steve does not own a place of his own to live. He has a passion for five-star hotels and has even resided in a few of them. Turning full circle, so to speak.Examining each one in turn.
In the year 2001, he is found to be in a terminal state at the W Hotel in Los Angeles. Behind the registration desk on the ground level, there is a human-sized fish tank that is always occupied by a stunning young lady. Thankfully, the tank never contains any water. She is donning a bikini as she teasingly pulls at the fluffy pile of turquoise hair and she is smiling. To the benefit of the eye-rolling males who are registering, this is all the better. Those of us who are huge fans of Fargnoli would argue that the whole environment has a strong Fargnoli vibe.
After this, I have no idea what will happen to any of us individually or collectively.
After they had finished saying their goodbyes to one another, his closest buddy Arnon entered the lift. At that same moment, there was a little earthquake.

Approximately seven seconds passed at that time. I am aware that he felt sorry for me. It makes no difference what the opinions of other people are. The poor man's heart was shattered by the tragedy. In the sand dunes. And the presence of God was with him.

SATURDAY NIGHT LIVE, PART ONE OF WAR, 1992

A little Irish pub can be found close to the intersection of St Mark's Place and Avenue A. It is owned and operated by a large Irish guy with shoulder-length grey hair who slouches because he doesn't think very highly of himself. But he's a decent human being. He is a good man. Even though he always dresses in black and has an air of dread about him, to the point that his face even resembles Ireland because of it, he loves his girlfriend so much that his face brightens up like England once she is in the room.

On the other hand, I despise Irish pubs. Nothing except inebriated individuals clinging to your arm, babbling incoherently, and weeping. Even if I don't like Irish music, one thing I do like is lighting up a cigarette. Therefore, I drink my coffee while sitting outdoors on the sidewalk and cross my fingers that the jerk officer with the silly Prince Albert moustache who once knocked a joint out of my hands won't come up. It is said that when he is not on duty, he may be seen sniffing cocaine in the apartments of the prostitutes that are located above the stores. It would be best if he didn't kick the checkers and just kept the joint for himself.

One night about one in the morning, I look out the window and see that just across from the Irish pub, a new juice bar has opened. A sign posted on the pavement indicates that the establishment is open even into the early hours of the morning. In a striking contrast to Ireland, I see that there are brightly coloured paintings hanging on the walls, as well as piles of fruit that appear happy, such as oranges and apples, stacked up by the pay register.

It seems like the folks who are inside are laughing quite a bit. So I gather my belongings, and I set off. Massive spheres of flame! I come across a number of people with long hair from the West Indies who are smoking pot on fresh tobacco leaves while listening to Rastafarian music. Forget the Irish pub; from now on, you'll be calling the juice bar 'home'.

After that, the only reason I go to the Irish pub is to rapidly refill my coffee, and I do it only when I need to. The West Indians will not go twelve feet across the road in order to enter the Irish bar. They do not have faith in the American people. Additionally, they have a negative opinion of coffee.

At first, they believed it to be a young man. When everyone found out the truth, there was roaring laughter throughout the whole establishment. It just so happens that I tell everyone one night that Robert Downey Jr. Is my true love. After I unzip my coat and pull up my jumper so that they can see my mangy Dunnes sports bra and pregnant stretch marks, the shocked silent faces that recited biblical phrases about the wrongness of homosexuality become sources of laughing. I am equally scared at being considered to be a man, so I open my coat and pull up my jumper so that they can see my bra.

Regarding Rastafarianism, it is very clear that I am an ignoramus. The manager of the 'juice bar' was the first person to address me, and his initial comment was that 'not everyone with locks is a rasta'. Additional laughter. But as time went on, he demonstrated his point to me. He goes by the name of Terry. He hails from the island of Saint Lucia. We are both of the same height. Hair that is long. It is a dark sallow colour, the same colour as peanuts that have been roasted. She has informed me that someone in her family has a history of having sexual relations with a "Chinese man." I tell him that we have something in common, which is the fact that someone in my family had sexual relations with a Spanish lady, which is the reason I am so pale and unhealthy looking.

I had hurriedly moved to New York from London during the winter, but for some reason I had forgotten to bring a coat with me. I was as cold as ice. Terry got in his car, went all the way to his home, and came back with one of his for me. A very large

Parka made of black leather. It is far too huge for me. I was completely submerged in it. Everyone of the young men laughed at me. But I adore it more than any Chanel outfit could ever hope to get. Simply because he owns it.

He is now the one who instructs me. I did not request that he be there. Because I wouldn't stop asking him questions about Rastafari, he decided to take up the challenge. Sometimes, I can tell by the way he tilts his head back and stares at me in a bewildered manner that he is pondering the following question: "What is God attempting to teach me through these questions?" But I'm not sure why you feel the need to ask that. My stomach is in knots. He has an awful lack of composure. Continue to fold the t-shirts and behave as if the establishment is nothing more than a juice bar.

In the early hours of the morning, he drives me around the fringes of New York City to eat ackee and salt fish with elderly Jamaicans who work in a variety of professions including butchering, fishmongering, and grocery shopping. There are usually one or two worn-out couches and a makeshift kitchen "backstage" in his retail storefronts or concrete warehouses.

Although not all elderly men wear dreadlocks, the vast majority do. In my estimation, they fall somewhere between the ages of forty and seventy. There is never a count of less than three. Together, they wait for the evening to come. They don't go to sleep at all. It is not necessary for God to shake you up and ask, "Won't you keep me company while I am insane?"

They don't waste their time with small conversation, Jamaicans. This causes some initial awkwardness due to the fact that Irish people have a habit of filling in the blanks. Just as when I was with my grandpa, I have to make deliveries while sitting silently in vans that are full of fish.

I concluded that they did not like me and chose to avoid conversation with me as a result. On the other hand, it boils down to a simple lack of observation. They are keeping a watchful eye on God in every place. They serve as though they were God's personal bodyguards. This is how people perceive themselves to be, and it is also how they really are.

They are analogous to Michael the Archangel, who leads the angelic armies of God into battle against Satan. As though billions and billions of Saint Michaels were coiled together on a massive bonfire of prophesy. They are keeping an eye on the devil as well. That being opposes God and his purposes. Your Lee Harvey Oswald is the devil in disguise. They only engage in conversation while discussing the Scriptures.

As they offer me plates of food under their tents, they address me as "Sistah" or "Da-taah" and say their names in unison. They advise you to "sit small." They are concerned that I am not eating enough. Never in my life have I been much of an eater. My adrenaline is pumping too quickly. The senior population often abstains from eating meat in favour of other foods such as fried fish, sweet potatoes, rice, and peas. Rice and peas is a dish consisting of rice and beans that have been cooked together in coconut milk. The very finest food that one can consume. I am relieved since peas are one of my least favourite vegetables, with the exception of when I am playing the game in which each player stuffs a frozen pea into one nostril while keeping the other nostril closed. The winner of the game is the one who is able to expel the pea the farthest.

The elderly folks have trouble pronouncing Ireland. They refer to the area as the land of Irie. They read from the prophets of the Bible known as the Nevi'im, but I ignore them and make fun of them. Despite the fact that I have a hidden love for eating, I still experience the same humiliating anguish from my childhood whenever I am hungry. He has far too many ties to my mother for me to ever accept him. In my mouth, the food turns to gravel, much as Lot's wife did when she turned around to gaze at him. I struggle, almost as though to demonstrate that I am completely dependent on God.

However, the wise ones are correct. They place an emphasis not just on eating, but also on excellent food. They refer to me more as a wooden spoon, and when they see that i've wiped the dish, they giggle gently in the back of their throats with joy. In point of fact, they take care of me like a lost kitty. They claim my moustache is as white as theirs, which is a compliment.

When I put my faith in them, they choose to instruct me. They carry it out in such a way that I am oblivious to the process. Do not put me in a chair and proceed to tell me this, that, or the other thing. They behave in this manner as a direct result of the topics of conversation that arise between them whenever I am around.

They talk out loud while reading from the book of Revelation about how this is the last chapter in the history of religion. Joyously bouncing about and laughing out loud. As if the prophesy had already been realised, they started yelling "Hah!" and "Rastafarian!" and "I fear!" while raising their arms over their heads.

The only thing they draw my attention to is a conversation about Ireland. "H-Englan is the natural adversary of H-Irie-lan. " What part of it don't you get? My response is that one would have to blind yourself to not notice it. They inform me that one of my grandfathers is a devil. Therefore, Satan himself is our true adversary.

According to what they have told me, "Jah's dwelling will be in a land among the race of men."

A artwork of Rastafarians may be seen hanging on the wall of Terry's juice bar. At the very conclusion of a lengthy cathedral floor that is tiled in black and white, there is an altar. On a massive golden throne that is covered in Amharic writing, a slender ebony monarch with the most affable face one could ever imagine sits. On each side of the room, there are greying males with black complexion seated along the floor. Cloudy with fog. You are unable to determine who they are. Lions, or those with ancient spirits. At the base of the throne, there is a little lady dressed in a white robe who is facing the emperor. His right hand is extended in a gesture of greeting. She is extending an invitation to him to visit the town. Because the dais is so much higher than her, she can only go up to her knees. He settles back into his chair, leans forward on his elbow, and juts his chin forward slightly as he does so. Kindly smiling at them. His head is shaved, and his skin is as white as snow.

One day, when I was in New York City to rehearse for Saturday Night Live, I was staring at the picture when Terry abruptly waved everyone away except for me. I was the only one left there. After that, he shuts the door to the store, swiftly draws the curtains, and then he asks me to sit next to him on the floor. As he puts my hands in his, he has a sorrowful expression on his face. I understand that you have something to say to me. He has told me that he hopes I would be able to forgive him.

He has informed me that they are planning to execute him in the near future. He claims that someone attempted to take his life earlier, when he was riding in a moving automobile. He was riding in his automobile with a few other people at the time. A different automobile drew up next to them, and seven shots were fired at the vehicle. He claims that they will capture him in the end.

When I ask him why, he gives me an explanation that I just can't take. He deals in both firearms and illicit substances. He has been transporting things with the help of youngsters. They are not carrying textbooks but rather guns and illegal substances in their school backpacks. It's just a matter of time until someone confronts him about moving into their area.

I can't believe he has acted in such a despicable manner and that he is going to be put to death. Throughout the course of the week, there is a consistent routine that takes place at the juice bar. On the Friday night in question, he gave it to me as a gift. It was a gold ring set with a red oval stone onto which was carved the head of a Roman soldier.

You're a damned scoundrel and a liar. I am capable of doing it myself. Even if they decked themselves with such a piece of jewellery, not a single Rastafarian on the face of the globe would dare to touch seven thousand pounds of grass that bore the image of a Roman soldier. I give it over to another Rasta, Rufus, who, upon receiving it from my hand, inquires in a perplexed manner, "Why?" He believes that maybe I am referring to romance. No. That is to say, the soldier seems to be him. The fool believes that this is a complement to his intelligence! I had no idea what the rabbi in London meant when he told me, "Don't forget to leave the party before everyone gets drunk and starts fighting." However, in that nanosecond, I realised what he meant. I go up the three steep stairs leading to St. Mark's Place from the shop, turn left into Avenue A, and then try to flag down a taxi. The driver implores me to give some thought to having sex with him while gently clicking his tongue against his back teeth in the manner of a person calling a dog. Where exactly do you think we are going to carry it out? I have no idea. Not in the driver's seat, that's for sure. It would be an understatement to say that you've had far too many burgers recently. "American XXXL" is the subject of our conversation. I tell him that i've had a terribly boring evening and that's why I can't do it. As we make our way through the bright lights of Manhattan and into my other realm, where I pace the polished floors of my hotel room till six in the morning, he performs the song "Underneath the Mango Tree" to me in an effort to cheer me up.

WAR, PART TWO: I HAVE TO SERVE SOMEONE On the day that my mother passed away, my brothers and I came inside her home for the first time in a number of years. We were shocked to see how much had changed. We have our own mysteries to solve. It is not hers. Broken pieces of plastic swans could still be seen in the lavatory. Resolved.Long in the neck.Frozen. As if nothing had taken place.

I took the one photograph that he had up in his bedroom, which was of Pope John Paul II, and removed it off the wall. This photograph was shot on his trip to Ireland in 1979. After acting as though the journey had been too terrifying, he had pretended to kiss the ground at Dublin airport and then remarked, "Young men from Ireland," adding, "I love you." What a load of ridiculous rubbish. Nobody had any affection for us. Not even God could change it. Even our parents couldn't take dealing with us, and that says a lot.

In 1978, Bob Geldof tore up a picture of Olivia Newton-John and John Travolta on Top of the Pops because their mediocre album "Summer Nights" had been number one for seven weeks before ultimately being overtaken by Geldof's Boomtown Rats track "Rat Trap." on. On.

My plan all along was to get rid of the photograph that the Pope had taken of my mother. It was a symbol of abuse, lying, and lying people. People with nasty hearts like my mother were the only ones who would have preserved these items. It was a mystery to me when, when, or how I would destroy it; all I knew was that I would do it when the moment was ripe. Keeping all of this in mind, I made sure to transport it properly to each of my subsequent residences after that day. Because nobody in Ireland cared a rat's rear end for the children there.

I went to bed at six o'clock in the morning and woke up at twelve. It is now one o'clock in the afternoon. There are barely a few hours left till the camera rehearsal for SNL. I'm going to play two songs, and the second one is going to be an a cappella version of "War" by Bob Marley. The lyrics are originally taken from a speech given by Emperor Haile Selassie of Ethiopia to the United Nations in New York in 1963. The speech was about how racism was the root of all conflicts in the world. However, I'm going to alter a few phrases so that it reads more like a declaration of war against the abuse of children. Because of what Terry said to me the night before, I have a grudge against him. The fact that he has been employing minors to distribute narcotics infuriates me.

And it really pisses me off that he'll be gone by Monday at the latest.

I've been reading The Holy Blood and the Holy Grail, which is a contradictory and profane history of the early church. However, i've also discovered brief essays hidden in the back pages of Irish newspapers. Both of these things have contributed to my anger over the last several weeks. About children whose lives have been irreparably altered by priests, but whose accounts of those events are not believed by the authorities or by the bishops to whom their parents complain. As a result, I have been giving considerably more consideration to deleting the picture of my mother that was taken in JP2.

I come to the conclusion that the time to act is now.

I go to the NBC studio in order to conceal the photograph, and I do it in the dressing room. When I finish singing "War" by Bob Marley at the dress rehearsal, I bring up a picture of a Brazilian street child who was slainby the law enforcement. During the performance itself, I request that the camera operator blow up the photograph. I don't share with him my plans for when we meet again in the future. Everyone is in a good mood. A youngster who has passed away in another country is nobody's concern.

I am well aware that if I proceed in this manner, conflict will ensue. But it doesn't matter to me. Scripture is not a mystery to me. I am immune to all influences. I do not accept the world. Nobody will be able to do anything to me that I haven't previously experienced myself. I'm back to singing out loud in public places like I used to. It's not like my throat was torn out of my body by someone.

It's time for the show. I'm wearing a white lace dress by Sade that formerly belonged to someone else. When I was nineteen, I attended an auction in London specialising in rock 'n' roll memorabilia and purchased it there. Eight hundred pounds was the price that he paid for it. It is quite beautiful. A lead weight around the size of a penny is attached to either side of the aperture at the back in order to keep it hanging correctly and in a ladylike manner.

Extremely astute. A garment that encourages ladies to act inappropriately. It's possible that one day he'll have a daughter who will end up marrying him.

Therefore, the show must go on. The opening song on the album is titled "Success Has Turned Our Home Into Failure," and it describes a dream. After the show was over, there was a large crowd of people milling about backstage, including producers, managers, make-up artists, and other visitors. I am now the most popular thing going. Everyone is eager to have a conversation with me. Please explain how i've been such a wonderful girl. However, I am well aware that I am a fraud.

The arrangement of the second song is very lovely. I sing "War" without any accompaniment a cappella with a candle at my side and a Rasta prayer cloth wrapped over the microphone. Nobody has any reason to suspect anything. But after it's all said and done, I don't have the photograph of the kid. I take the photograph of JP2 in my hands and then proceed to rip it into bits. I scream in their ears, "Fight the real enemy!" (I am addressing the individuals who are responsible for Terry's death.) And I extinguish the candle by blowing on it.

The crowd was completely speechless due to their shock. When I go backstage, there is not a single person that I can see anywhere in the area. Every door in the building is now locked. They are all nowhere to be found. Included among them is my own boss, who shuts the door to his room, disconnects his phone, and stays there for three days.

Everyone, as you can see, aspires to be a pop star. But I consider myself to be a protest singer. I just needed to get some things off my chest. He had no interest in achieving famous. In point of fact, this is the reason I went with the first song. "Success" was turning my life into a miserable failure. Because everyone was already telling me I was crazy for not behaving like a pop star the way they expected me to. For not being obsessed with gaining recognition. I am conscious of the fact that I have dashed the hopes of individuals in my immediate environment. However, they are not the dreams I have. Nobody has ever questioned me about my goals; instead, they have just been angry with me for not conforming to their expectations of who they thought I should be. My personal goal is to fulfil the agreement I made with God before I signed any contracts related to the music industry. And that's a battle that's preferable than killing someone. I have to look at things from a different perspective.

Ciara, who works as my personal assistant, and I am now in the dressing room. After gathering my belongings, we exited the facility. Two young males are waiting for me outside of 30 Rock, and as soon as they see me, they begin hurling eggs at both of us. They are unaware of the fact that Ciara and I are both capable of sprinting one hundred metres in eleven and a third seconds. Therefore, when they flee from us, we chase after them. They were in some back alley when we found them. They are struggling to catch their breath as they lean against a tall, dark fence that they were unable to scale due to their lack of muscle. The only thing we can think to say to them while laughing at them is, "Hey, don't egg women." The two are so taken aback by being pursued and captured that they start laughing, and the situation resolves itself in a fairly amicable manner. They helped us straighten up and get a cab so that we could go back to the hotel. The issue is being covered in the news, and it has come to our attention that I have been permanently expelled from NBC. This bothers me, but not nearly as much as the rapes that were committed on those Irish children. To say nothing of Terry's death. Which occurs the Monday after the previous one regardless.

IT'S NOT NECESSARILY SO

MANY PEOPLE say or think that tearing up the Pope's photo derailed my career. That's not how I feel about it. I feel like having a number one record derailed my career and the fact that I tore up the photo put me back on the right track. I had to make a living performing live again. And for that I was born. I wasn't born to be a pop star. You have to be a good girl for that. Do not worry too much.

I wasn't comfortable with what other people called success because it meant I had to be the way other people wanted me to be. After *SNL* it could just be me. Do what I love. Be imperfect Being angry, even. Anything. I don't define success as having a good name or being rich. I define success by keeping the contract I made with the Holy Spirit before I made one with the music business. I never signed anything that said I would be a good girl.

I have supported my four children for thirty-five years. I supported us by playing live and became, if I may say so, an excellent live performer. So far from the Pope episode destroying my career, it set me on a path that suited me better. I'm not a pop star. I'm just a tormented soul who needs to yell into the microphones from time to time. I don't need to be number one. I don't need to be loved. I don't need to be welcome at the amas. I just need to pay my annual overhead, blow off steam, and not compromise or whore myself spiritually.

So no. It didn't go off the rails. He was re-railed. And I feel like i've been very successful as a single mom supporting her kids.

THE STATE OF CONDITION MY CONDITION IS IN THE FOLLOWING: 1992, after a few days had passed, I arrived to the Chelsea Hotel early this morning and checked in. It just so happens that none other than Dee Dee Ramone resides there, and he comes on my door bearing not a cake or cake but some acid pills, and he asks if I'd want to partake in whatever it is that he's doing there.

I keep my mouth shut and don't tell him that it's the first time i've ever done it, downloading one tab while he consumes another. It has come to my attention that you are very underweight. It seems that he does not place any more importance on eating than I do, which is not surprising given that he does not at all. We are aimlessly roaming around the streets of the city, going in a direction that we are unsure of, and dancing to the music that plays in different cabs that we pass. At one point, we even push our head in the open window of a driver who is stalled in traffic and shouting at the top of his lungs at Ella Fitzgerald. He displays the front cover of the CD for us. She is beaming and dressed head to toe in pink. As my Aunt Frances instructed me to do, I take the cover in my hands and read all that is printed on it, even the reverse side.

It's obvious that this isn't Dee Dee's first rodeo when it comes to getting high, and her priorities are all jumbled up as a result. After sitting there for a couple of hours, she eventually finds a step to sit on and begins behaving in the same manner that Sybil did in the film of the same name about multiple personalities, "The People, The People, The People." He is under the impression that everyone is looking at him. They are not, and even if they are, it is only because she seems to be on the verge of losing consciousness. He makes the decision to return to the Chelsea Hotel and then abandons me completely. It makes no difference to me how things are set up. It indicates that I am at liberty to go to St. Mark's and Avenue A. Which I will, of course, do.

At Terry's place, I catch up with an old friend who is a rabbi. I am not familiar with his given name. Because he is continually talking about God, people have given him the label Rabbi. He has the appearance of a Rastafarian, yet he is a very furious person despite having that appearance. He does not qualify as a bonafide rastaman. In point of fact, it wouldn't shock me if he got rid of a few individuals. He has a vindictive nature that runs through him. There are moments when I ask myself why I continue to hang around with him. I believe the reason is simply because he is fascinating. Together, he and I went to the park. There is still daylight outside. I often find myself smiling at people I don't know. Acid is similar in this regard. It restores your innocence and makes you more receptive to the company of others, just like you were when you were a kid. A blonde lady gives me a kind grin in return. Sitting with her spouse or doing whatever else she was doing. When Rabbi begins stroking my hands in a manner that makes me think he may want a spin or two on the leaba (Irish for "bed"), I realise that it's time for me to leave him and go back to the Irish bar. I couldn't care less. Regarding him, I do not have such feelings. Who would want to share their bed with someone who is always so grumpy?

  After that night, I decided that I would wait until I was 33 before using acid again. I was with my buddy BP Fallon, who is a radio personality in Ireland, at a rockabilly club on London's Oxford Street. He is a huge fan of rockabilly music. I can't take it any longer. Therefore, I'm pleading with him to let us leave the club now. He is certain that we cannot go at this time. After one hour, I'm totally clear-headed, which leads me to believe that acid is a bad choice. Comparable to the quality of music. And I grab the full bag of acid from Beep (his nickname is Beep), lock myself in the bathroom, and take it off as he thumps on the door and threatens to murder me on the way out of the house. Beep's nickname is Beep. As I devour each and every tab in the bag, I can't stop giggling. Despite this, I'm as alert as a magistrate once another hour has passed. Nothing is taking place at this time. Beep has most definitely been taken advantage of, since they are only a few little cardboard cubes and not acid at all. However, he does not leave the club, and the two of us wind up remaining there for a total of three hours. Finally, at near midnight, he gives us the okay to go.
  Whoosh! That's what happens as soon as my right foot steps onto Oxford Street. I am in the air. Because I detested the music so much, it hadn't caused me to trip. It wasn't until tonight that I realised how profound my connection is with music. I was laughing so hard that I was crying, which is one of my favourite feelings in the world, and I was mesmerised by the stars. Let's get together and start a fire at my place, shall we? When you're under the influence of acid, the flames of a fire

may seem to be formed of worms. It is the strangest thing imaginable. It makes me question whether, behind closed doors, everything is really constructed out of worms. In the off chance that she chooses to take me up on my offer, I can't stop myself from throwing open all of the windows and inviting the outside into the home. Of course, it will never take place. We didn't stop chatting until far into the night. At one point, I look over at my piano, and all I can see is the word "monster" where the arrangement of flowers had been moments before. The flowers resurface and begin twirling about as soon as I recognise that what I'm seeing is only a fabrication of my imagination. Therefore, I became far better at controlling my thoughts when high than when I was sober.

I have experimented with ecstasy on a few occasions. It retched my soul. Cry the next day for the mother of anybody. Contracted into the shape of a foetal ball.

The same goes with coke. Two times, in fact. It retched my soul. The next day I woke up sobbing like a cartoon; however, instead of running down my cheeks, my tears were shooting straight and horizontally. There is nothing redeeming about it. I'm down in the dumps and twenty bucks poorer. It is not even remotely worth the effort. He adopted my social mannerisms.

When I was younger, I used to smoke heroin. That is really reprehensible. I resolved never to do it again.

The next medication that I tried was speed. In the nuthouse, which, believe it or not, is located in Dublin (I refer to it as a nuthouse due to the fact that I am a nut). Nobody else may refer to it in such manner). There are a greater quantity of medications classified as Class A in the locked room where you are taken if you are having suicide thoughts than there are in the dressing room that Shane macgowan uses. They never inspect the baggage that guests bring into the building. It is not like in the United States, where even your grandmother would be searched against the wall and ejected if she brought you a bottle of perfume to give to you as a gift. That being said, i'll be there for a whole week, and it will most likely be one of the happiest weeks of my entire life. The same thing happened after two years. A week long bender inside the locked chamber of the mental institution. It inspired me to put pen to paper. In this very moment, I really wish I had some. But despite how much I enjoyed the class, I resolved that I would never take it again.

My relationship with alcohol has never been a friendly one. I have an allergy. I simply had to throw up. I believe that I must be the sole Irishman in the whole world who does not consume alcohol. I was probably twenty-three years old and living in New York the last time I got drunk. On Saint Patrick's Day, at the Fitzpatrick Hotel, plywood had been attached to the bar floor in order to protect the carpet from the vomiters and noisy paddies who had travelled all the way from Ireland only to become drunker than the skunks. These Irish tourists had travelled to the United States simply to drink more than the skunks.

It was Irish coffee, but with those horrifying crème de menthe shamrocks sprinkled all over the top. During the whole night, as the world swirled around me and I threw up, I clung to the toilet and held it. And despite my extreme exhaustion, I was unable to fall asleep due to the quantity of coffee I had consumed. The next day, I was still sick to my stomach. Since then, I haven't had so much as a sip of alcoholic beverage.

I am incredibly fortunate since I was able to give up all of these substances with quite little effort.

It was marijuana I used while I wasn't fully alert. He never stopped working while he was on the lawn. And I enjoyed it because it allowed me to retreat into my own universe whenever the real world seemed to lack any coherence. The majority of artists like cannabis due to the fact that it inspires them to create music and helps them get through long stretches of sitting around doing nothing. Additionally, it makes sitting around doing nothing intriguing. Hotels, changing rooms, buses, and airports; they work for two and a half hours a day, and the rest of the day is spent waiting incessantly.

Indeed, I couldn't get enough of the grass.

MAN LIVING ON THE STREETS AT EASTER

THE MOST OUTSTANDING HUMAN BEING THAT I HAVE EVER COME IN CONTACT WITH WAS A HOMELESS PERSON WHOSE NAME I DID NOT EVEN RECALL. I apologise in advance if any of it rhymes. It wasn't long before my debut on Saturday Night Live, and I was at a restaurant in New York full of white folks before the holiday of Good Friday.

This African American guy walked through the door while donning a long, long trench coat in the style of a military uniform. Around his neck, he had a jack-to-jack wire, which is a cable that links a guitar to an amplifier.

While I was seated at the bar area of the restaurant, all of the other white customers were seated in the booths throughout the remainder of the establishment, and this guy did not belong among them. Therefore, the manager of the establishment him around and escorted him out, which caused me to experience a great deal of amazement since an event like this would never take place in the nation in which I was raised.

The next minute, or perhaps closer to five minutes later, he arrived back to the house. And he performed what I believed to be the single most extraordinary act that a person is capable of doing. After returning to the eatery, he stood around six feet inside the establishment with his arms extended wide and said, "Can I have a hug? Could you give me a hug?

I thought you were a genius. And as soon as I saw him, I raced up to him and pounced all over him like a monkey. In addition, I was the only individual who completed the task. I ran into his arms and clung to him like a newborn, putting my legs around his waist and huffing and puffing like a child. I spent a good deal of time clinging to him.

After that, we stepped outdoors to have our discussion there. After we finished talking, he handed me the jack-to-jack leash that he had been wearing around his neck. I don't recall what we discussed.

It was misplaced during one of the many moves that took place in the home at some time. But for a very, very long time after that, it served as one of my most valued possessions. It was hung up on the wall in the bedroom that I was using. And he is often in my thoughts. What a stroke of brilliance it was to ask, "Will you give me a hug?"

It never comes to an end. The loudness was the most intense i've ever experienced. It felt like a sonic uprising, as if the sky itself was splitting apart. It makes me really queasy and comes dangerously close to bursting my eardrums. And for a minute or two there, I'm beginning to wonder whether or not the people in the crowd are going to start a riot. They are already competing with one another so vigorously with their voices. How am I to know what other possibilities exist?

I spend some of my time on stage walking. I have come to the realisation that if I begin the song, I am doomed to failure since the voice is so soft that the audience members on both sides will be able to drown me out. And I can't allow myself to be ignored because those who jeer will see it as a sign of success.

I am looking at the dashing face of Booker T. The words are being said by him. Sing the tune, but I won't be doing it myself.

Right now I'm talking to God about what I ought to do. I continue going, which makes things unpleasant for everyone backstage since the event has to go on as scheduled. Since of this, someone sends Kris Kristofferson (he tells me this later), and he is supposed to "run her offstage." As he walks in that direction, God reveals to me the solution to my question: I have to act in the same way that Jesus would. As a result, I rip up a picture of the Pope while screaming the lyrics to "War" by Bob Marley at the top of my lungs with as much fury as I can summon. After that, I came close to being ill.

I look up and see Kristofferson coming in my direction. I'm thinking to myself, "Thank you very much, but I don't need a man to save me." It is a terrible reflection on you. When I picked up my microphone, I heard him say, "Don't let the jerks bring you down." And as we leave the stage, he hugs me, and I feel queasy to the point where I nearly vomit up on him.

After the fact, I got the impression that Bob Dylan should have been the one to step up front and request that his audience let me perform. And it makes me furious that he didn't help me. Therefore, I give him a strange look, as if he were my elder brother, who had just informed my parents that I had missed school. He seems perplexed as he looks at me. He wears a white shirt and trousers, and he has a really dashing appearance. It's the most bizarre minute and a half of my whole life.

Following my visit to Madison Square Garden, I will pay Dylan's manager a call at his office the following day. I explain to him what i've learned about what's been going on in the church in Ireland, which is that children have been raped and the church is trying to cover it up. I inquire as to whether he and Dylan will assist in bringing it to light. He believes i've lost my mind. He makes no attempt to assist. Neither he nor Dylan is going to make a statement on my behalf. I am alone myself here. (I wonder whether they still consider me to be insane at this point.)

After the event, my father, who was there that evening, confronts me with the possibility that it is time for me to reevaluate my decision to not attend college in light of the fact that I had just ruined my career. He has a valid point. But it doesn't matter to me. There are certain things that are important enough to sacrifice a job for. And now that no one recognises me or cares about what I have to say, I have no interest in pursuing a career as a pop star.

MY BANNER OF THE STARS

THE REVERSE AFTER SNL was more powerful than it had been a couple of years previously when there was another scandal.

The year is 1990, and for the last several days, i've been staying in hotels where i've been able to see news video that has both brought tears to my eyes and made me laugh out loud. While i've been travelling around the United States, i've seen that in some towns and cities, individuals have started piling up stacks of my records at crossroads.

This has been the arrangement up until now: "Bring Us Your Sinéad O'Connor Album and We'll Crush It for You." Over the little hills of CD, we went ahead, then backward, then forward, then backward. Drivers of the steamrollers were elderly guys who were quite irate and had highly pointed noses. I can't remember the last time I laughed that hard at anything. Between sound check and showtime, I had the wonderful honour of participating in a protest against myself with my best friend Ciara. The Irish artist in me has never been more proud, but particularly today, when, while donning a pair of sunglasses and a wig outside the grounds of New York's Saratoga Performing Arts Centre, I had the opportunity to join Ciara in a protest against myself. We pretended to speak with an American accent as we engaged in conversation with the handful of Vietnam veterans who were the only other attendees at a demonstration organised by a local radio jockey.

They were, shall we call, "big," and they were all guys; three of them wore enormous circular black-rimmed spectacles with lenses that were so thick that it gave the impression that their eyes were enormous. They had painstakingly created and proudly displayed banners that made it clear that they believed she should leave the United States immediately and that ALL SINÉAD O'CONNOR LOVES ABOUT THE UNITED STATES IS THE DOLLAR. These banners left no room for ambiguity.

To point out that they were in the wrong is so obvious that I hope it goes without saying. It takes a fool not to love the United States of America. In addition to this, only a jerk would leave the United States for a cause other than to avoid being deported. In spite of the fact that I may be accused of other things, both rightfully and unfairly, my reputation as someone who is not an asshole is one hundred percent secure. More than ever before, because if I were a jerk, no one would need to be rolling over my records, and that would eliminate the need for anybody to do so.

This is a really positive development.

Ciara and I wholeheartedly agree with the demonstrators that "Shine-Aid O'Canerrr" and others like him need to "Git back to Eye-errr-layand." That "she is just a wicked woman trying to corrupt our keeyuds with her disrespect," among other things.And that "there is no way in the world that it could be Christian!" We even go so far as to snap pictures of them with us to put in their scrapbooks. They were overjoyed that two young guys who were such upstanding citizens had taken care of them.

After walking back and forth with the banners for around twenty minutes, the women eventually scaled a wooden fence and took a seat to observe the men as they continued to do their duties. A news team had arrived because in the preceding days, some parts of the media had been attempting to incite a significant demonstration by the general public. However, as it turned out, that plan was unsuccessful, and the men were the only demonstrators who were recording.

The next thing we know, a brunette TV reporter from the nearby station approaches us together with her cameraman and sound guy, the latter of whom is sporting an outrageously phallic fuzzy microphone on her head. She addresses the question to the speaker directly, saying, "Excuse me, miss, are you from here?"

I make the decision to draw out the "Uhhh" sound for quite some time. After that, I hazard a guess and say, "Ahhm frum Sarah-toga." Both Ciara and I are doing our best not to snort with laughter whenever we glance at each other. The reporter is curious and says, "Ewe de Watt nom-er?" "Uhh. My response is always the same: "I'd rather not give my name to complete strangers." We just narrowly avoided going over the edge of the barrier.

It's a good thing they got away soon. We were far too peculiar. However, some time later, it was printed in the newspaper under the heading "Is She? Play the video of my "interview" many times in a row. Aha-ha-ha-ha-ha!

When I was getting ready to perform a few of months ago in New Jersey, my dressing room was visited by a guy and a woman who identified themselves as Caucasians. This is how they refer to people from that ethnic group in the United States. Before my performance, I was asked how I would react to the playing of "The Star-Spangled Banner," which is the name of the American national song, over the venue's speakers.

Because English is the primary language in my home country, I interpreted the phrasing of your query and the fact that you offered it as a question to mean that you wanted to know if I didn't have a positive reaction to it. Please accept my apology for this misunderstanding. That is an excellent idea. What, no national anthem? It's not an issue.

Just between the two of us? Unless Jimi Hendrix is performing them, anthems almost always conjure up images of a square, and this connection may be horrifyingly infectious. In addition, the majority of people go to events in order to forget about the outside world, not in order to recall it while they are there. But I only had about 10 minutes till it was time to go on stage, and I wanted to get the wires down the back of my shirt and do the last of my typical panic pees, so I simply remarked that, if given the option, I would rather it not be touched. I did not provide them any kind of justification or explanation. They greeted him with a warm grin and encouraged him to "have a great show" by praising his "very good" performance.

But it turned out to be an incredible set-up all along. While I was performing, the two manganes contacted a local TV news programme and falsely reported that I had sought them out and demanded that the anthem not be played before the concert. This caused an outrage throughout the country. While I was on stage, the manganes did this. In addition to that, they made certain that I informed them that it would come to an end if it was played. That assertion is completely deficient. Because I'm not a jerk, I won't be a jerk and tell you that your travel insurance policy won't cover such a choice.

An uproar in the media follows. Sinéad, the one who despises the United States of America. During the most exciting part of my journey.

Making a big display of sending me a cheque for a first-class ticket back to Ireland, MC Hammer attempts to capitalise on the situation. The bill, just as he does, has an aroma of coconut. I am even able to recognise that he is an arrogant businessman in his own right. In the future, the item's value will much exceed the one thousand five hundred dollars that he originally set it at when he wrote it.

Actually, now that you mention it, there is a cause to leave the United States, and that reason is the MC Hammer films. Christ, the All-Powerful.

Frank Sinatra interrupts us and tells us that we should "kick our asses," which is unsettling considering we are both staying at the same hotel. We could run into each other in the lift, and I'm not sure how well it will go down with my father in Dublin if I have to tell him that I had to fight Old Blue Eyes in order to protect myself.

I start looking under my mattress for severed horse skulls.

I'm thrilled that the Establishment thinks me to be enough of a danger to attempt to discredit me along with all the other bands and musicians who have been under assault in this music censorship that has been going on in America ever since Straight Outta Compton. I'm flattered that the Establishment considers me to be enough of a threat to try to discredit me. Evidently, we have all stumbled onto the correct answer. It is quite clear that we have all been participating all along. I am aware of what it is as well. We are comparable to the mirror that Snow White used.

PART THREE

SOME MUSICAL NOTES

I'M SURE PART of the reason I became a singer was that I couldn't become a priest, given that I had a vagina and a pair of (albeit insignificant) breasts. I have always been interested in working with the dying, because I have always been a person who strongly believed in the afterlife and in the lack of need to fear death, which I perceived because the Gospels had been instilled in me. I assumed that was the reason Jesus came to Earth. That seemed to sink in to such an extent that only now, as I write about my songs, have I realized that a lot of them are about death or talking to dying people or where the narrator is a dead person.

In fact, the first song I wrote, "Take My Hand," featured an angel singing to a dying old man, "Come with me. Everything will be rosy." It was an unusual subject to write about for a fourteen-year-old boy.

I have written a lot in this book about my upbringing and my youth and how I came to be an artist. But I haven't written much about the individual songs or albums yet. I thought it might be helpful to list all the information you can about them. I always say that if you could talk about music, you wouldn't need music, because music is for things you can't talk about.

Keep in mind that each album represents a journal and each song is a chapter of that journal. And my album collection represents my healing journey. When I was younger, I wrote from a place of pain, because I needed to vent. Once I got to the *Theology album*, which is all Scripture, I worked from a place of healing. And the first album that I wrote entirely from that platform is *I'm Not Bossy, I'm the Boss.* And it is from that platform that I continue to write. After all, there is no point in going on a healing journey if you are not going to find yourself healed.

And it also happens that if someone really wants to know me, the best way is through my songs. There is nothing I can write in this book or tell you that will help you get to know me. Every thing is in the songs.

WHAT I DO NOT HAVE IS NOTHING THAT I WANT TO HAVE

After composing "Take My Hand," the next song I remember writing was "JACKIE." I was about fifteen years old when I wrote it, and it was included in Lion and the Cobra. He had seen a drama on television about an elderly lady in Scotland who was in the latter stages of her life. She would spend her days peering out her curtained window, hoping to catch a glimpse of her late husband returning from a fishing trip he had done forty years previously and during which he had perished. The fishing excursion had ended in tragedy. They did not have any children, and she was never in a relationship with anybody else.

This in some ways motivated me to create the story "Jackie," which is about a character who lingers on the beach in anticipation of the return of a loved one who has passed away. The narrator of my song is a spirit of some kind.

People always believe that my songs are autobiographical, but in reality, this is only the case around half of the time. They are often incorrect in their assumptions, particularly when they believe a song is about a mental disease when it is not. Despite the fact that "Jackie" isn't actually affected by this at all. It is noteworthy to note that this song belongs to the group of lyrics that are performed from the point of view of persons who have gone away after their time on earth. Musically as well as spiritually, I was troubled by the fact that he appeared to have had an interest in the afterlife even back then, as well as a skepticism in the idea that death is the end of all.

It's all because, as I said before, I didn't have the chance to become a priest. Actually, a missionary would have been preferable, but music was all that was available at the time.

As I had previously indicated, the song "Drink Before the War" (I have no clue where the title came from!), was inspired by my resentment against the principal of Waterford High School, who despised the fact that I wanted to be a musician. The director was a snobby and cowardly little son of a bitch, and I didn't give a crap about what he did. When I was writing the song, it had a lot of significance to me, but I don't ever perform it because it makes me feel embarrassed; it's like reading the journal you had when you were a teenager out loud.

The song "Never Get Old," which was also written by me when I was around fifteen and included on my debut CD, is one that I continue to play. Ben Johnson, the school's most dashing young man, is the subject of this story. Because he was not only the most attractive person, but also the most mysterious, each and every one of the ladies want to have him as a boyfriend. He was a kind man who spoke very little and trained falcons. He was a falconer. As I said before, I was eventually able to go out with him one day. He brought me to visit him and his falcon, and we had the most incredible day together. I wrote about this experience earlier. I believe that at the end of it all, we had shared one or two kisses. And then they went their own ways, I have no doubt that he would consider it to be complete and utter hogwash. But as is often the case in these situations, when i've approached people with songs that I was afraid were complete garbage (such as "Reason with Me," which is about a person pleading for assistance with his life), people have appreciated them.

And despite the fact that I am not a very skilled guitarist, I was rather pleased with myself when I realized that I could play the guitar.

When I go back to the songs on I don't want what I don't have, I realize all over again how prevalent the concepts of passing on, dying, and connection with the hereafter are throughout the album. In the first tune, titled "Feel So Different," I really had a conversation with my mother. And the ancient Irish poetry known as "I Am Stretched on Your Grave," which is essentially about death, bears the title "I Am Stretched on Your Grave." I utilized the famous James Brown drum sound that was beginning to appear on a lot of rap songs; the record label had me pay fifty thousand for it, but I guess the money didn't go to James Brown's drummer. I used it since it was starting to appear on a lot of rap tracks. It's one of my favorite songs to sing, and whenever I do, I can't help but think about my mom. When I'm on tour, it's not uncommon for a celebrity to die away during my set, and when that happens, I always dedicate "Stretched on Your Grave" to the departed.

The song "Three Babies" is the third song about death, and it is about the three miscarriages I had. It is also about the four children that I had, despite the fact that the song may be a premonition of the fact that I was not the ideal mother. She has aspirations of being the ideal mother to her children, but it's possible that won't always be the case (even if she does grow better as she gets older).

The film "Black Boys on Mopeds" is based on a genuine tale that takes place close to where I used to live in London and involves two young teens. They had borrowed a motorbike belonging to a cousin without first obtaining permission, and when the cousins saw that they were being trailed by the police, they panicked, crashed, and were killed. This occurred around the time when there was a serious controversy in London about the disappearance of black males from police stations. In addition, there was a period in London when a thief who was apprehended would be referred to as a "black thief" (or, alternately, a "Irish thief") in the police record. On one side, the Londoners produced a lot of strain, while on the other, the Jamaicans and Irish added to the already existing tension.

My rendition of Prince's "Nothing Compares 2 U," which became the album's breakout hit, was a song that I used to sing to my mother all the time and still do to this day. When I am acting as her, I have the distinct impression that this is the last time I will ever get to spend with my own mother and that I am communicating with her once again. There is a notion floating about that she is there, that she can hear me, and that we may communicate with one another. Because of this, the statement that made me cry was "All the flowers you planted, Mom, in the backyard, they all died when you left." I felt so bad for the flowers. The song is one of my favorites, and I never get sick of singing it.

The song with the same name as the album, "I Don't Want What I Don't Have," was likewise delivered in a manner that was both foreboding and intriguing. My mother accompanied me and we went to visit a psychic. My mother begged my sister to forgive her for all that she had done to all of us and she finally accepted her request. However, my sister would never forgive her for that. When I finally realized this, I couldn't help but feel terrible sadness for my mother's eternal soul. I was so young, and I had no life experience, so I didn't know any different.

That night, I had a dream in which I saw my mother for the first time since she had passed away over a year and a half before. In the dream, we were together again. In the dream, I conveyed to my mother my condolences for the fact that Éimear was unable to forgive her. My mother was of the opinion that "I don't want what I don't have."

My mother was trying to get across the idea that she did not merit the forgiveness of my sister, and that she was aware that she did not merit the forgiveness, so that I would not feel sorry for her.

On both my first and second albums, there is a significant amount of content revolving around the concepts of death and passing away. But i've also observed, huh, that there are a lot of songs about believing in the spirit world; it's not just "Oh, oh, oh, these are miserable songs about death." There are a lot of songs about belief in the spirit world. This is not how it works at all. There are certain songs that are based on the concept that the Gospels are similar to that and that the Scriptures from the past are authentic. And that there is no such thing as death, as all of the prophets of God have explained to us, irrespective of the religious tradition from which they hail.

IS IT TRUE THAT I'M YOUR GIRL?

I WAS NOT READY for the kind of success that was brought on by I Don't Want What I Don't Have. I was hoping to find something else, but it wasn't there. I was at a loss on how to deal with it. He infuriates me to no end. I was puzzled as to why someone enjoyed listening to my tunes. When I was doing them in front of every camera in the world and on every television program in the world, I had no idea where I was; I was not with my kid. I was confused about my identity. I didn't feel like I fit into the mold of a pop star, and I didn't like what the role was doing to me.

Musically, I didn't feel like I wanted to put myself through the pressure of doing a normal follow-up album. I was in desperate need of coming up with a red herring. I came to the conclusion that it would be best to purchase some time in order to complete the next album according to my own artistic vision, rather than the one that was required by the record company. No one would be able to compete with a red herring follow-up record because it would be so far afield from the standards set by the pop industry. So I did just that with the song "Am I Not Your Girl?"

Show songs and jazz standards populate the whole of the record. The only piece that has any kind of personal touch from me is Loretta Lynn's classic song "Success Has Made a Failure of Our Home." Because I am really the one talking about how my life has changed as a result of my accomplishment. In the end, I came up with certain terms that were highly autobiographical and used them in my writing. After the song's words had finished playing, I all of a sudden began shouting, "Ain't I your girl?" It was the only portion of the record that I believed followed "I Do Not Want What I Haven't Got," and it stood alone.

In addition to that, I covered the song "Don't cry for me Argentina" since it was one of my mother's favorites growing up. And the fact that I was able to sing it brought tears to my eyes. A letter I got from Tim Rice, who penned the lyrics, telling me that my rendition was, without a doubt, the finest he'd ever heard meant the world to me. He said it was the best he'd ever heard, period. And if my mother hadn't already passed away, I have no doubt that she would have done so full of happiness and pride.

The track "Scarlet Ribbons" can be found on the album. It was a song that I remember my dad singing to me when I was a little girl. That is the reason why I am sobbing while singing it. It has such a profound and important importance to me. The fact that my dad sang that song to me also served as a powerful reminder of the transformative potential of prayer and the miraculous outcomes that are possible. The song's backstory left an incredible impression on me. When my daughter was little, my dad would make her cry with his sad singing voice, much as he did when I would sing to her. I think my dad had a terrible singing voice too. My songs would come on the radio, and whenever he heard them, he would exclaim, "That's sad, turn it off, turn it off."

MOTHER OF THE UNIVERSE

I OFTEN THINK ABOUT UNIVERSAL MOTHER AS BEING THE MOST SPECIAL ALBUM THAT I'VE EVER MADE, AND ONE OF THE REASONS WHY IS BECAUSE IT HAS TO DO WITH MY FATHER. A guy by the name of Frank Merriman had been giving me vocal lessons for a number of years. He was known for instructing students in the bel canto style of singing. It was first used in Italy at the beginning of the 19th century and literally translates to "beautiful singing." It has absolutely nothing to do with scales, breathing, or anything else of the kind. The idea behind the entire thing is that emotions are what push you to the notes. I sung with an American accent while I was making my first two albums in London, where I was living at the time. I attempted to sing in the style of all of my musical heroes. I never sung under my own name. In the 1980s, singing with an Irish accent was considered very offensive, and Bob Geldof was the first person to do so publicly.

I didn't start singing with an Irish accent until I went to see Frank Merriman when I was a student. I did this because I used to have dinner with him and my father quite frequently while my father was in Dublin, and I was extremely pleased with what he had to say about singing. I didn't start singing with an Irish accent until I went to see Frank Merriman when I was a student. He referred to himself as a freer of voices rather than a singing instructor, and he characterized singing as a spiritual study, which, in his presence, it really was. He was a freer of voices. Studying with him resulted in the first time I sang with my own voice, and I was able to speak things that were genuinely going through my head without having to encode them as much as I had on prior albums. This was made possible because I was able to sing with my own voice for the first time. Frank liberated not just my voice but also my thinking, and I am grateful. When it comes to bel canto, one element cannot exist without the other.

The key of the opera arias that Frank had you perform, such as Puccini's "O Mio Babbino Caro," was too high for you to sing. Just as he was getting to the point when you knew you were about to put on an amazing performance, he would toss you an apple or a tennis ball, and you would be so preoccupied with trying to avoid it or catching it that you would miss his high note. Meaning that the note would exit your body once it was played. It was the Stanislavski style of singing, and it was his way of demonstrating to you that you were just in your own unique manner. If you were able to get out of your own way, tell the narrative, and experience the sensations, then the notes would be on you. When there was a fire, Frank would tell everyone, "If a fire started in this room right now, you could yell Fire in the highest octave there is." However, if you attempted to sing that note when there was no fire, you would never get close to reaching it.

Therefore, seeing the sights, telling the tale, really believing it, and having faith that the notes will bring you to the emotions are the essential components of bel canto. Nothing related to learning how to breathe, nothing related to the diaphragm, and nothing similar to that is involved in this process. Because everyone's muscles develop by the age of fourteen, and these muscles generate the sound of your accent, it follows that you will end up with vocal issues if you limit your dialect. The only technical component is that you must always vocalize with your own accent. Because of this, you can see Bono, you can see Adele, and you can see some musicians who have taken on a faux accent and who have vocal difficulties because their vocal chords have constricted so that they can perform in a manner that they are not designed for.

I came back to Dublin in 1993 so that I could continue my vocal training with Frank, both individually and in a group setting on Saturdays. There were around twenty persons in each of the group courses. A few of them just wanted to perform at social gatherings. A few of them had aspirations of becoming professional singers. Some of them simply wanted the delight of coming to a singing class (like my father did), where you would learn that everyone's soul is unique and beautiful, but the ring in everyone's soul doesn't come out until they're singing in their own way. This is something that you would learn there. Own genuine manner of speaking. And that is what makes it so incredibly lovely.

I learned a technique from Frank that I occasionally employ on stage, and it was via his instruction that I learned it. During the performance, i'll be thinking about my foot and kicking it while at the same time. I'm not going to let myself think about the notes I have to sing because, if I do, I'm going to mess up. So I'm not going to think about the notes. I try to distract myself from the grades I need to get by thinking about anything else.

It was through these classes that I became aware of the significant commitments and efforts that a person's passion for singing might require of them. Frank is a guy who, when he was younger, traveled to Italy and, since he was unable to afford a place to stay there, he slept on a park bench for a whole year. Only enough money for him to study had he saved up. Later on, thank God, he went back to Dublin to work as a teacher there.

As i've already said, Frank was the one who first began instructing me on how to sing in my own voice and discover my own soul. As a consequence of this, I began talking about the topics that I had been most interested in discussing, and in the meanwhile, am I not your girl? Despite the fact that it was technically my third album, the title was misleading. Even though I sung about my background in songs like "Lion and the Cobra" and "I Don't Want What I Don't Have," I hadn't really talked anything about it. Now, the course of events would alter.

This reminds me of the film Universal Mother, which was released in 1994. Phil Coulter is a nice guy who is responsible for producing the most of the record. Nine of his children were born exactly nine months to the day after he got home from tour. As a child, Phil looked up to Geraldine Brannigan as a singer, and now the two of them are married. Phil is a very talented pianist. In addition, he penned the song "Scorn Not His Simplicity" that is included on the CD.

One of the things that makes me so proud of Universal Mother is that Edge, from the band U2, has said that he can only listen to it once since it is so personal. The same thing that Nigel Grainge stated about the record that "Nothing Compares 2 U" is on, which I talked about before, is that he said, "I don't want what I don't have." He compared it to reading the private journals of another person while knowing that no one would object. I guess poor Edge experienced things in a different way. It was more that he felt all of the sorrow that he had built up inside of him. Universal Mother was also the album that was given the finest review that has ever been given to one of my albums. This review was provided by the late Bill Graham for an Irish publication called Hot Press. His assessment said that it was the first time anybody had ever sang about his family, and that the topic of family had always been taboo. However, as an artist, it was precisely what I had been working for all along in order to accomplish it. That was exactly what I had in mind, but of course, by this point he was singing with a different accent and behaving like a whole different person. Everything was encoded with an extremely strong password. And it was quite clear that this was a delicate young lady who was not necessarily the tough Bambi dressed in combat boots that everyone believed she was.

Now, I have to confess that I have never been as high in my life as I was when I was in Amsterdam with Tim Simenon, who created the songs "Fire on Babylon," "Famine," and "Thank You for Hearing Me." Now, I have to say that I have never been as high in my life as I was when I was in Amsterdam with Tim Simenon. Jesus, a lot of cannabis being smoked in this house. I don't even know how I was able to sing; I can't even explain how I managed to remain upright.

The song "Fire on Babylon" was written about my mom. It was something I found out she had done to one of my brothers that really infuriated me, but I won't go into too much detail about it since I don't want to give anything away. The fact of the matter is that I find it difficult to feel resentment against my mother. It's the only way i've managed to stay alive. I was able to persuade myself that she was not competent in the task at hand. People will act in such a manner, but naturally, i've moved beyond that anger, and maybe it would be more mature for me to accept it at this point. You can even see how angry I was with her in the film when I presented the poor mother figure with a birthday cake that exploded in her face. I did this to make her feel bad about herself.

"John, I love you" is one of my absolute favorite songs. I adore absolutely single aspect of it. Although many people believe that I composed it about my brother John, that is not the case; yet, there are occasions when I do identify it with him. This is the history of the situation: John Stokes, a piano instructor at Frank Merriman's school, was the one who introduced her to the piano, and she fell hopelessly in love with him. Because he was pretty smart and he understood that I was utterly insane, that I was the last woman any guy could want for himself, of course he wasn't interested in me at all. He was quite sensible, and he knew that I was. Despite this, we were good friends, and I loved him a great deal—in fact, I loved him an incredible amount. I was never good at playing the piano, and to this day I still can't. When it comes to playing the guitar or the piano, I really use my elbows instead of my hands. (It's far more difficult with the piano.) Anyway, John Stokes is the subject of the song, and it was written about him.

The song "My Darling Child" is about my son Jake and was written by myself. Just a love song and a lullaby for you. "Am I a Human?" is obviously Jake's contribution to the record, for which he has a publication deal, and it can be found on the album. He was probably only around three years old when he strolled up to a microphone at his father's home, and all of a sudden, this astoundingly profound philosophy gushed out of him.

This album was the first time in my life that I became myself, and it was the first time that I started to fully realize what I had been in the first twenty-two years of my life; I was finally coming to terms with it. "Red Football" is a reference to the fact that I was finally coming to terms with it.

People believe that Daniel Day-Lewis and I had an affair, but that was never the case. The song "A Perfect Indian" is about him. The friendship was on the verge of being restored until I lost my cool with him one night and acted in the irrational manner that I often do when I do things like that. Because of this unfortunate consequence of my upbringing, the song is just as much about me and my background as it is about Daniel. The fact that he was filming The Last of the Mohicans at the time inspired him to give the song its current title, "A Perfect Indian." It's not that she had feelings for him at all. (He was not.) [Not] On the other hand, I cherished our friendship tremendously. Despite the fact that I have only seen him once in the last twenty-five years, we love one other very deeply to this day.

My mind was utterly blown at the one and only revival session i've ever attended, and the song "All Babies" was the reason why. Even though I had never been on an acid trip before, it felt very much like one, and it was the most enchanted experience i've ever had. This song was also a major inspiration for the painting that is included on the CD, which is the only cover artwork i've ever created. This leads me to wonder: where exactly is the original drawing? It's possible that it got misplaced somewhere in the bowels of Chrysalis or EMI, or that it was sold, but whatever happened to it, I'd really appreciate it if I could get it back.

My relationship with Peter Gabriel came to an end, and I created "Thanks For Listening To Me" as the last track on Universal Mother. She and him had been involved in an on-and-off affair, and the term "weekend fag" would be the most kind way to characterize his role in the relationship. And when I finally grew sick of being a weekend fag, I decided to write a song in the style of a breakup ballad. But over the course of the years, it evolved into my favorite song to perform live because it had the ability to transport you, much as a mantra would, into these higher realms that were almost hypnotic.

I believe Tim Simenon was the one who provided me with the background music. Everyone in the band, including each individual line, the bass line, the drums, and the audience, would be mesmerized by the repetition of it. When asked to explain the inspiration for the song, I have a hard time doing so. Playing it, for want of a better description, is somewhat of an ecclesiastical experience in and of itself. And I am very, very proud of it as a breakup song, given the fact that one is allowed to smash dishes when they discover that their significant other is treating them like a weekend faggot. I am very, very pleased of it as a breakup song.

I remember going on a TV program in London and attempting to perform that song in the thick of the political tensions between Ireland and England; they told me that I shouldn't play the song because it was too political. With regard to "Famine," yeah, I remember going on that show and trying to sing that song in the heart of the political tensions between Ireland and England. My mother and father informed the director,

"But hold on. You wouldn't argue that he is incapable of performing "The Times They Are a-Changin'" if he were Bob Dylan. There was no one who could do anything other than agree. In the end, we were successful in getting it shown live at least once on British television. The song "Famine" is, of course, about Ireland and how everyone thinks there was a famine in Ireland in the 19th century while, in reality, there was loads and tons of food in the nation; it was simply being transported out of the country. The song also discusses how everyone believes there was a famine in Ireland in the 19th century. The problem was that if you were Irish and approached any food that wasn't a potato, you were asking to be killed.

The claim that there is a famine is not supported by the facts. It was a contentious song, but if I hadn't written it, I never would have connected with the father of my daughter, who has written such lovely things about her. His name is John Waters, and we decided to talk to each other about an interview about that music. Roisin, our daughter, would not have been conceived had we not done those things, and had that song not been written.

GOSPEL OAK

Oak of the gospel he got his name from the area of london, united kingdom, where he went to see a therapist on a daily basis. Morton schatzman was the name of the extremely elderly jewish psychiatrist, and his dog had the peculiar habit of sitting at his feet and licking his testicles. As i sat there attempting to explain what was wrong with me, the situation was really uncomfortable for me. What i enjoyed most about dr. Schatzman was his statement that the purpose of treatment is to discover that there is nothing inherently wrong with the patient. When his dog began licking his balls, though, i knew there was something very wrong with me. I'm irish, so to say the least, i felt a bit uneasy about the situation.

But i was really, extremely fond of this guy, and in many respects i may have even been passionately in love with him, as a patient is often with his or her therapist. And at that time, he was the only one who was courteous to me. Because he suffered from severe loneliness, he visited the establishment six times a week. It's possible that my challenging personality contributed to my feelings of isolation. I was too young to comprehend the information at the time. Also, i suppose, for the sake of my employment.

Despite this, "this is to mother you" is the only song on the album outside "all babies" that was written by itself. There are occasions when creative people would state that they get the impression that they are channeling something. I don't have that impression at all. In any event, the voice that you are hearing is probably that of your subconscious, which is communicating with you. Also, you need to be extremely cautious about what you write because every songwriter will tell you that the things they sing about eventually end up happening in real life. I simply happened to hear it inside of me, so i picked up the guitar and started singing it.

All of the tunes on gospel oak were created using a similarly subconscious approach. The song "i am enough by myself" was written as a reflection on the subjects we were discussing in therapy at the time. It consisted of my sitting quietly and repeating a series of positive statements to myself about the way i envisioned things in my life.

The song "petit poulet" was my visceral response to what i witnessed on the news about the massacre in rwanda, and the song "4 my love" is just what it sounds like: a love ballad. The song "this is a rebel song" was created in reaction to "sunday bloody sunday" by u2, which the band typically opened during their concerts by saying "this is not a rebel song." "this is a rebel song" was composed in response to "sunday bloody sunday." it's possible that they were concerned about how people would compare it to the conflict in northern ireland. And he wanted the audience to understand that this song was not only about love; rather, it was a song about conflict. But how exactly does one go about telling the tale of a war? It would be beneficial if you could make it appear as if you are discussing the connection that exists between a man and a woman.

On this album, you'll also find the song "he moved through the fair," which is also often referred to as "she moved through the fair." it's a hauntingly lovely traditional irish tune, yet no one can place the song's authorship. I rerecorded it in a somewhat higher key for the michael collins movie, and i truly enjoy that version of the song just as much as the original.

Due to the fact that we toured both albums together, gospel oak and universal mother will always have a strong association with me. Those excursions were where we had the most fun of our lives.

FAITH AND COURAGE

Faith and courage, which was my fifth original album and my first original release in a significant amount of time, was released in the year 2000. Creating the album was a creative and invigorating endeavor on many levels. It had been a challenging period of time. While i was taking care of jake and roisin, i became embroiled in a terrible and miserable custody struggle for her, and on the day i turned 33, i made an attempt to take my own life.

I developed wonderful working ties with a number of the producers of faith and courage, most notably adrian sherwood and dave stewart. In point of fact, i was in a relationship with adrian sherwood for a considerable amount of time. I would collaborate with adrian on anything; if he were recording the phone book, i'd sing every single entry in it. He is the most fantastic producer in the world, as well as the finest joint builder; if i were to construct one for him, i would adorn it with cute tiny love notes.

Both "thank you for hearing me" and "the healing room" are examples of the same kind of music that can be found on this album. People may perhaps be transported to another universe by reciting this phrase. When i walk on stage, i always hope that i will be able to serve as a priest, and that when i leave, the audience will have the impression that they have just come from a religious service. The song "the healing room" has a calming and soothing effect on me.

"no man's woman" is a typical example of a pop song, while "jealous" is one of my absolute favorites. I collaborated with dave stewart on the music, and it ended up being one of my all-time favorites.

Additionally, dave said to his father, "dad, i'm doing fine." dave had given me instructions to go and compose a song on the experience of moving to london. I really like doing it live because you are required to yell and shout the whole time. "hold back the night" has one of the most impressive vocal performances that i've ever given. It was written by bobby bluebell of the bluebells, and dave stewart discovered it for me to perform. I don't believe i could have found anything finer to sing than that song.

Wyclef jean and i worked on "dance lessons" together. That was a wonderfully enjoyable experience. After engaging in some light banter with me for a while, i finally felt compelled to tell him, "don't waste your time."

The record label insisted that "the state i'm in" be included on the album faith and courage. I detest it in every possible way. It was not written by me. This is not the sort of music that fits with who i am as a person. I had always been instructed by frank merriman to never sing a song that wasn't in my personality, yet here i went and sang it anyhow. In addition, i can't help but feel angry since i believe he ruined the record.

During the time that i was in the united states recording a portion of the album, "the lamb's book of life" was produced by she'kspere briggs. She was unaware of how miserable she was when she was in atlanta; he probably thought i was the most boring biatch in the world (and i definitely was), as a result of all the issues i was experiencing in london and ireland.

However, the account that is told in "the lamb's book of life" is really about that horrible time period.

My mother passed away when i was young, and the song "if u ever" is an imagined discussion that i had with her before she died. "emma's song" is about my connection with john waters, my daughter's father, who i mentioned previously, and "kyrié eléison," well, that was just for mischief: a rastafado rendition of the first portion of the catholic mass. Both of these songs were written by john waters.

The fact that there were so many talented musicians and some of the most talented producers engaged in the development of faith and courage contributed to the positive experience i had. As i've said before, the fact that i was high the whole time prevents me from recalling many specifics. Working with so many diverse creative minds included a degree of risk; thus, the fact that everything ended up working out is nothing short of incredible to me. The only song on this album that i don't like is "the state i'm in," but other than that, i couldn't be more pleased with how it turned out.

SEAN-NÓS NUA

Some of the very greatest songs that i've ever written are included on fe y valenta. The next cd, sean-nós nua, which translates to "old new style" in gaelic, has some of the finest songs i've ever sang.

It was an eerie record because there are a lot of traditional irish songs that no one recalls who wrote them, so i feel like they're ghosts; in order to bring these songs to life, you have to embody the character of the song. The album sean-nós nua was created in the most eerie settings possible, and the production of the album was surrounded by the most bizarre of occurrences. We recorded at a really peculiar home out in the country, and there was a tree nearby that was what people in ireland refer to as a haunted tree; in fact, it was very close to being an evil tree. The house's only kid, a very young infant, passed away not long after we finished recording the cd. It was a pretty tragic situation. Of course, they are all melancholy tunes, since no one in ireland is capable of writing a cheerful song worth a damn.

Despite this, the tracks and the cd as a whole are rather lovely. Shane, who is my third kid, was also produced by dónal lunny. If we hadn't done this album, we never would have had the opportunity to have our wonderful son. I also persuaded adrian sherwood to contribute his time to this album once again due to the fact that none of the traditional irish tunes had ever been reggaetonized.

The song "peggy gordon" is one of the most beautiful of them all, and we purposefully played it in a very high pitch to make it seem even more melancholy. And no one has ever sang "the moorlough shore," "molly malone," or "the singing bird" in a more impressive manner than this man. I am well aware that boasting is a terrible sin, and i fully expect to spend eternity in hell because of it, but this cd is very, extremely amazing.

I believe that i am still a decent vocalist; nevertheless, i will never be able to sing as well as i did when i was a member of faith and courage and sean-nós nua. I had reached the optimal age for it at the time.

Additionally, my connection with dónal lunny was ideal from a musical standpoint. As a producer, he has excellent intuition; our collaboration was outstanding, as was that of the band and the record label. Everything went off without a hitch. It seems to be aimed towards a certain section of the market. The album spent a considerable amount of time at the top of the charts in ireland.

THROW DOWN YOUR ARMS

In 2005, i had the good luck to record the song "throw down your arms" in kingston, jamaica, with sly and robbie (sly dunbar and robbie shakespeare), along with the most incredible band on the face of the earth. I was given the opportunity to sing a number of incredibly manly rastafarian songs, which are among my all-time favorites and provide me with the greatest motivation. I had the best three weeks of my life in kingston with a very jovial buddy of mine; at the time, being homosexual in jamaica carried a penalty of 10 years of hard labor. I had the time of my life in kingston. Because of this, i had to keep caressing my friend's chin in order to get him to keep his lips quiet whenever he stared at the attractive males. And he was having an affair in our hotel room, which we shared, with one of the hotel waiters, and the poor waiter kept mistaking me for my friend's wife the whole time they were having the affair in our room.

We had a lot of fun while recording at tuff gong, creating some excellent songs and smoking a lot of pot. My relationship with robbie shakespeare blossomed into a beautiful love, and we had some incredible experiences together. After that, when we went on tour in support of the record, robbie and i had a spacious bed in the rear of the tour bus. We couldn't get enough of those programs, but our relationship was our first priority at the time. In point of fact, he was fond of every member of the band, and they referred to me as mother since i looked after them so well.

It doesn't matter how sad i am, "prophet has arise" by throw down your arms, which was created by the renowned jamaican reggae band israel vibration, is my favorite song because it lifts me off the floor and makes me feel better. Later on, i was given the opportunity to sing with israel vibration at brixton academy on one of the nights when my good buddy benjamin zephaniah was singing there. It was a really poignant event for me. It was an amazing experience to be able to sing along to all of my favorite israel vibration songs while holding the hand of the band's lead vocalist. Because i have such a deep and abiding admiration for him, i paid tribute to the jamaican roots artist burning spear by covering a good number of his songs on throw down your arms. A very valuable lesson that i picked up is that you should never, ever leave your marijuana in the dressing room while there is a group of rastafarians around; it will be gone when you come back for it.

To tell you the truth, i was feeling really down when i recorded "throw down your arms." my life has been filled with unfavorable experiences recently. It was one of the factors that led to my entry into the spiritual realm. I was also so persuaded to make throw down your arms that i funded the creation of the album out of my own pocket, which cost me a total of $400,000 dollars. I was working on my next record, which was going to be called theology. If you can believe it, i'd been thinking about recording that album ever since i was seven years old. Throw down your arms served in many ways as a predecessor to theology, which was also funded by my own personal contributions. (i don't recall how much i had to pay for it).

THEOLOGY

Around the year 2000, i attended college for a few semesters with the intention of majoring in theology. My interest was mostly focused on the books that were written by the prophets. When he was talking about the prophets, we had the most wonderful instructor, who was a priest. He was able to remove god out of the equation when he did this. Especially jeremiah; he would be crying, "my poor people, my poor people," while tears would be streaming down his eyes.

He sought to remove god from the composition in the same way that he did while he was lecturing; in other words, he wanted to do the same thing musically. Everyone should be able to perceive the human side of god, including his frailty, his bad temper, and his emotions.

When the instructor walked in, he touched the book with his finger and remarked, "you should be writing songs about that." at the time, i was reading the song of songs in silence while i waited for class to begin. And in this way, he was the source of inspiration for my album theology; i had really been considering it for a very long time, but i didn't know how to put it into practice. When it comes to composing religious music, there is a thin line between being cheesy and being amazing, and i grew up in the 1970s with all of these dreadful charismatic christian tunes on the airways. As a result, i chose not to take the chance of making that error.

Only one of my albums, "theology," will accompany me to my last resting place when i die. It's wonderful! I used almost all of the letters that are found in the bible, and i recorded one side with just an acoustic guitar and a vocalist and the other side with a whole band since i couldn't decide which version i loved more. Different renditions of the same songs. My method of working consisted of laying out large sheets of paper on the floor and writing down all of the verses that i admired from the scriptures. Then, i decided to put them all together and not alter the verses in any way, but instead try to make them rhyme wherever possible. In addition, god has already provided us with several wonderful songs that are recorded in the scriptures.

The first track is titled "something beautiful," and it recounts a genuine tale of a time when i stole a bible (which i believe should be freely available to everyone). It also explains why i wanted to compose the album in the first place. While "out of the depths" is taken from one of the psalms, "something beautiful" is the sole passage that deviates from the general portrayal of all of scripture.

The song "dark i am yet lovely" originates from the book of songs. The passage from the book of isaiah that contains the phrase "if you had a vineyard" the song "watcher of men" comes from the book of job, which is notorious for its challenging rhyming structure and lengthy running time.

My rendition of "the rivers of babylon" for "psalm 33" is a little different from the one most people are used to hearing. And i adore my rendition, not because it was written about me, but because it is lovely, the lyrics, the emotion of people breaking their guitars because their tormentors demand music. This is not the most welcoming of the psalms. It seems like there will be a lot of babies and all that.

Psalm 91 refers to "he who dwells" in its title. I was taught the psalms in the jewish tradition, which teaches that there are mystical applications of the psalms and specific ways to employ them in conjunction with the names of god. Psalm 91 is a shield that protects against harm. The record label was relentless in their pursuit to have me include "i don't know how to love him" on the album. Although it's one of my favorites, this is not the appropriate place for it. My selection of "we people who are darker than blue" was equally unwise.

Graham bolger, who is a friend of mine, and steve cooney worked together to make theology. Graham had been involved in a tragic accident at the time (it was really on my birthday), in which he had fallen from his motorbike, crashed, and became a paraplegic as a result of the incident. I encouraged him to stay at the cottage that was attached to my property, and he accepted my offer. Because he was going through a very difficult and depressed period, it was beneficial for him to gather everyone together and work on this album. Graham, steve, and i were able to come together every day and produce the music, which helped graham realize that life was going to carry on despite his illness. Graham is someone who i still consider to be a very dear friend and whom i love very much; we all had a very lovely experience while studying theology, which is another reason why it continues to be so very meaningful.

It gives me such joy to play these songs live. And just as i said before, if i end up in a coffin, it will be the only record i take to heaven with me in the hopes that it would make up for the total piece of garbage that i am the rest of the time.

WHAT IF IT'S ME?

It took me a few more years to create my second album, titled "how about i be me," since i was taking care of my children throughout that time. I began composing songs from a different platform; at first, i wrote about the suffering i'd experienced throughout my life, including my childhood. When i first began writing, all i did was write songs, and some of them were based on screenplays. Take for instance the song "far far from home," for which they provided me with the narrative and for which i composed the tune. However, i did not wind up handing it over to the movie in the end. I just did not tell anybody else about it.

The children's movie the water horse, which starred emily watson and was about the loch ness monster, had a song called "back where you belong" written for it. I provided it to them, and while they made use of it, i retained a copy for my own records. Daniel lanois was in charge of the production, and we did the recording in my home in monkstown, which is located in dublin. Daniel is a character who is very sensitive. The last time i saw him, i was really worried about him because he was playing the guitar at a performance without a plectrum, and as he came offstage, his fingers were sliced into strips, actually deep wounds, and he was bleeding and bleeding. I was very concerned about him. I inquired as to what was wrong with him, and he informed me that his brother had passed away not long before. The unfortunate man's life had completely fallen apart.

Daniel is a really trustworthy person. There was a time when we attempted to record a version of "mind games" by john lennon, but i was unable to sing it very well. There are certain songs that i simply don't have the vocal range for. Daniel was really forthright and honest with me over it. I like his candor, which is one of his many strong points. The fact that he does not kiss your ass is a commendable characteristic in a producer. And he's quite kind about the whole thing. When you're either the artist or a woman (or both!), some producers may be quite controlling. These producers want to say everything, and they want to meddle with your lyrics and other aspects of your music. However, daniel would never act in such a way. It was never easy, but i appreciate all of your help very much with the challenging task that we performed together.

"take off your shoes" is one of the songs that i'm the most pleased with that i've written. In this day and age, when there are so many allegations of scandals involving the church, it is about the holy spirit communicating to the pope and the vatican. It was done with the goal to blaspheme. I find the concept of a spirit singing or of me performing in the role of a spirit to be really fascinating. The true name of this singing technique is the frank merriman/stanislavski method.

I also had the opportunity to sing "queen of denmark" by john grant. This song is the most enjoyable for me to perform live since it contains the finest chorus of any song ever written: "i don't know what you want from me." when they hear the chorus, the crowd goes completely ballistic.

"reason with me" is a stunning song that discusses the experience of being a heroin addict. To say that i am a drug addict is an understatement; the fact is that i am a drug addict. This song is about the struggles of being a drug addict as well as a fuckhead. Because i couldn't be bothered to speak about the songs on this album when i first released it, i pretended at first that none of them were autobiographical. However, each one of them is.

Except for the first song, "4th and vine," which in no way reflected the artist's own life and was not even really autobiographical. It occurred as john reynolds was playing a background track, and all of a sudden, i saw a picture of brides running into their own ceremonies. Therefore, there are times when the songs are just about nothing, and there are other times when i write about topics that i feel strongly about expressing.

The process of songwriting for me begins and ends with me. I have never attempted to create a song by sitting down with a guitar in front of me. As i go about my day, whether i'm cleaning the home or walking down the street, i find that tunes come into my head and start singing to me. One day, a portion of the song will play itself for me to sing along with. The next week, the subsequent portion of time. The next week, the subsequent portion of time. Because of this, i've never actually attempted to sit down and create a song in the traditional sense. I simply let them grow inside of me like a tiny building, and when they are completed developing inside of me, that is the time at which i will sit down with a guitar.

The controversy around the how about i be me album cover continued. I was dismayed to find out that my management and the record business in britain did not think it was appropriate to make use of the exquisite artwork of the girl seated in her nightgown on top of the irish flag. I was upset by this news. (the european union edition has just a single picture of myself.) Nevertheless, i didn't have much of an option but to give in and permit it. It was really my first album that wasn't just about me, that wasn't just adolescent angst or young lady anguish, and it wasn't just about any of those things. Even though some of the songs aren't quite upbeat, it's important to remember that i was creating them for other reasons, about other things, other people, and other places.

It represented a turning moment, which i believe began with sean-nós nua and throw down your arms and theology; they were stepping stones for me to get to a position where i didn't have all this dreadful shite that i wanted to get off my chest. It marked a turning point, which i think began with sean-nós nua and throw down your arms and theology. Consequently, it is the meaning that i get from this album.

I'M NOT BOSSY

My previous albums were kept on a daily basis since it was necessary. It's not that i'm bossy; i just am the boss it's so close that i nearly consider it to be my first album. These were just pop tunes and love songs that lasted for three minutes. It is interesting that the opening tune on this album is titled "how about i be me," which was the name of my last album. He was intended to go there, but it was already too late for the professors. Therefore, i decided to add it, "i'm not bossy," since i like that saying. At first, it was a reggae song; someone had given me the reggae background track, and i wrote it down; but, in the end, i decided that i did not like it in a reggae manner. The song "dense water deeper down" was written as a love ballad. In point of fact, it was brian eno. The song "kisses like mine" was not written for a specific person. I have no idea where the idea originated; i was simply playing the guitar and strumming when it occurred to me.

The album's producer, john reynolds, was the one who gave me the background music for "your green jacket." this is a fantastic song that is all about something that young women do: sniffing one other's clothing. If you love a guy, you would be sniffing his shirt or his jacket all the time. This is a sign of true affection. I have no doubt that males do the same thing. People get the impression that it borders on stalking, but i don't believe it goes as far in that direction as adele's song "someone like you," which includes the lyrics "i was hoping you'd see my face and remember that for me, it's not over." i accomplished something with 'the vishnu room' that i had never done before: i wrote a lengthy song that exposed the sort of woman i am capable of becoming. I don't think i've ever truly written songs that are vulnerable. I have also heard statements to this effect made by other musicians. Take, for instance, amy winehouse. She said that he probably shouldn't have recorded his own funeral for the "back to black" music video. She mentioned this herself.

"take me to church" is a song about songs and how what you write in songs comes true, thus you need to be extremely cautious about what you put down on paper. The protagonist of this song is penning lyrics about how much she loves the guy featured in the song. Finally, she succeeds in tracking him down, and his extreme panic can be heard in the next song, which is titled "where have you been?"

Finding romance, falling in love, receiving what you want, and then realizing that you want to run away and hide for a million miles is an unusual type of trip. But this shouldn't make you feel down. It's a pop album, and all of the songs are love songs. It's gorgeous, and i'm so very proud of it.

COMING SOON . . .

I thought this might be an opportunity to speak a little bit about my next album in the summer of 2020, which is the one that i'm working on right now. But before i continue, allow me to take a step back.

The nurses had informed me that mr. X, a patient at this chicago veterans administration hospital, was a "difficult" patient, but in reality, he is not at all tough. Simply put, he needs access to the internet. Her eyes are virtually blind because she has been sobbing so much over the loss of her son, who committed suicide a few years ago, that the bottom edges of her eyelids have riverbeds in the midst of them. It boasts the largest television that i've ever seen in a home. Literally speaking, it ought to be ninety-five inches high. He is able to get up and move about thanks to a line that is threaded through his nose and into a giant white oxygen machine that is positioned on the ground next to the chair he is seated in. He suffers from emphysema. Life expectancy with smoking. (i can tell that it will most likely turn out the same way).

She says that she does not have any fear of passing away since she is certain that she will one day be reunited with her son. She also mentions that she has been at the hospice for the last six weeks, despite the fact that she did not want to enter the facility. It is bustling with activity. You would have no idea that you are passing away at all. And i don't inquire with anybody, not even him, about the amount of time he has available.

He is ninety-two years old, originally hails from syria, and served the united states of america during the korean war.

It's been 10 years since the death of his wife. He shows me some stunning photographs of them when they were younger. In the pictures, they are dressed up for an evening out dancing and seem to be having a great time together. He has a son who is still alive, but since he lives on the other side of the nation, he is unable to be by his father's side while he is in the hospital.

Consequently, i'm responsible for it for around one hour every day at the present.

He is a participant in a program that goes by the name "no veteran dies alone." companion on the trip towards death for troops whose families have passed away or who simply do not have any family members around due to some other circumstance.

I make an effort to connect him to the internet, but i am unsuccessful. Why the veterans affairs facility doesn't have wireless internet access is a mystery to me. Your television may as well be a fish for all the amusement it provides, since all you have is my ugliness to look at instead.

There is a second elderly guy who tells me he looks forward to my presence in the foyer each day because i perplex him. He is a veteran who served in vietnam. Also the number ninety-two. Because i often visit the hospital dressed in a babe ruth baseball uniform, he is unable to determine whether or not i am a male or female. In addition to that, my head has been shaved. The guy is completely taken aback by this information. He has been waiting for me again this morning, which is the morning after he discovered that i am a girl. He then says, "so, are you a lesbian?"

"i do not tell him. "then why would you take off all of your hair?" even though he is absolutely perplexed by the situation, he continues to wait for me every day since he has never previously seen a straight lady who is hairless. He is unaware of the fact that i do not identify with any sexual orientation. I don't even bother lighting him since he's already in such a state of panic that it would be pointless.

I am also responsible for the care of a woman who is ninety-two years old. During the second world war, she worked as a driver. She sits there for the whole of the day drawing images of disney princesses. I get him some chunky markers that have faces on them. The employees take them right in front of me, and that horrifies me every time.

When i push her about in her wheelchair for her walks, she stops acting like a little disney princess and instead reverts to the role of a grown-up soldier. He does not speak, but he indicates to me with his head nods where the snipers are located on the roofs of the hospital. True. For the sake of safety.

So there is no internet, but there are people who shoot people. When there is no fighting going on. What a mystery.

When i quit my job (which is voluntary) to go back to ireland, fortunately, none of my children, whether they be males or girls, pass away. This is by far the most enjoyable and thought-provoking position i've ever had. As a direct consequence of this, i have a profound admiration for service members.

In recognition of the program, the title of my subsequent album will be no veteran dies alone. I've just finished writing the main tune. I am going to make it my own tribute to mr. X. In addition, during the autumn of 2020, i want to begin training to become a health care assistant. This is going to be my other source of income in between tours and making albums, and it will enable me to be with terminally ill patients. For many years, this has been a goal of mine to achieve this. I'm going to see to it that it happens now.

DAGGER THROUGH MY HEART

My favorite collaboration that i ever recorded was "dagger through my heart," which i performed on a dolly parton tribute album where she picked the vocalists. This song is my all-time favorite collaboration that i have ever recorded. Because he thanked me and complimented my rendition of his song later on, i hold this one in the highest regard. This is the primary reason why it is my favorite. I had the letter framed, and then i presented it to my stepmother viola as a present. Because both she and i are huge fans of dolly.

As i sat on the beachfront porch of my home and looked out the door, as is my usual routine on a very early summer morning, i found myself reflecting over the previous week. Then, an elderly lady with white hair that was cut short and unkempt came strolling up my driveway with her dog. Her face was crimson, and she seemed to be quite agitated as he waved an empty water bottle made of plastic in front of her and asked if he may fill it up for his dog. It seemed as if he was having trouble breathing. The elderly woman said that she was experiencing a panic attack. As a result, i found a seat for her and prepared a cup of tea for her, all the while dolly's song kept playing through my thoughts.

He suffered from a heart problem and had just overheard some troubling information from a stranger on the boardwalk, which caused his heart to beat quite quickly. She said that even though she is able to work over her sorrow, it is still difficult to do so when you are aware that a loved one is going to pass away in the near future. We sat there for much over an hour. She was quite pretty. Constantly apologizing despite there being no need to do so. Without my knowledge, she was really the one who was helping me out.

The day before yesterday, she arrived back. With her hair styled and feeling like "herself" once again. Therefore, the more i thought about it, the first time i saw her, i realized how sad she was. I started from the very top and worked my way down to the basement. She assured me that she would do the same thing and then presented me with a stunning white handkerchief. I believe that i like reading dolly's letter just as much as i enjoyed reading it. In addition, i have high hopes of running into her once again since she is a truly remarkable person. I can't tell you his name, but i'll give you a hint: he's featured in a song that i've performed.

However, she is aware of her identity, and i would want to express my gratitude to her. There are a lot of strange people that come my way. Almost never does an angel.

THE GREATEST LOVE OF ALL

When i was a very young boy, the boxer muhammad ali was both my greatest idol and my biggest source of motivation. My father woke me up at least once in the middle of the night to see one of his most famous bouts. In addition to that, i saw a lot of video of him in fights on tv, and i would look at it every time he was featured on the news. Watching people fight was never something i enjoyed. It bothered me to see black guys beating one other up for the pleasure and financial advantage of white men, and i didn't appreciate witnessing it happen.

In addition, since i was a victim of child abuse at the time, i found it quite upsetting to witness the fights. Despite the fact that i sung throughout the conor mcgregor bout, i continue to be opposed to the concept of using violence for entertainment purposes. I pressed his mother's face into my chest so that she wouldn't have to see what her son was doing to her, regardless of what he was doing to the other people. Ali was much ahead of his time when it came to affirmations, and i admired him because we shared similar struggles with low self-esteem as african-americans. I'm sure that all child abuse survivors felt the same way about him. We arrived there by a different route, but once we were there, we were still held in a type of slavery (with an apostrophe). I am aware that using the term "slavery" to describe what it is like to be a survivor or a victim of child abuse may cause some people to question whether or not they should apologize for doing so; but, the fact of the matter is that the word has been used.

Anyway, let's go back to the point. Ali was able to go into the homes of irish children and explain to us that our parents were in the wrong. He did this by reaching out to everyone. In our nation, sinful behaviors such as running about yelling things like "i'm the prettiest, i'm the biggest, i can do whatever i want, i'm so beautiful" were considered to be unacceptable not just for those who had survived childhood sexual abuse but also for practicing catholics. Because believing that you were an unworthy sinner was a prerequisite for being a good catholic. That was the concept behind it. The less you focused on yourself, the more god would focus on you as an individual. Therefore, ali was able to enter our living rooms, utterly demolish the theocracy, and even destroy the... What exactly would you name it? I have no idea. The democracy of young children? He demonstrated to us that we were, in fact, really attractive. We could have been saved, and we could have been redeemed.

In addition to this, not only were we the largest, but we also stood out as the most beautiful. In addition to that, it demonstrated to us that we were going to do something worthwhile with our lives. That despite all that had occurred to us, we were going to get ourselves up off the ground and go on. A few decades ago, his daughter laila, who is also a fighter, gave him an interview. I remember hearing that interview. Someone inquired of him, "do you believe in god?" he said, "yes." what she said in response, which nearly brought tears to my eyes, was that "all i have to do to believe in god is look at my father." and i'm sure it not just captures how the rest of the world felt about him, but also how he felt about his own father.

Aside from giving birth to my children, meeting muhammad ali was without a doubt the most incredible event i've ever had. Not only did i have the chance to speak with him, but in 2003, my eldest son jake and i accompanied him to the special olympics that were held in dublin. And that is how the event transpired.

In dublin, bon jovi had performed, and the event had been so loud that the neighbors had complained about it. You could even hear the show where i lived, which was around twenty miles from the venue. And someone phoned me and said if i'd want to attend to the after-show party, which i did, and it was held in a hotel in dublin called berkeley court, which used to be where all the important people would stay when it was first built.

As soon as i arrived at the party, i struck up a conversation with heather, who was jon bon jovi's wife at the time and a really beautiful woman. And i tell her how much i like muhammad ali, and she's like, "oh my gosh, we're meeting muhammad ali tomorrow, because he and nelson mandela are hosting the special olympics here." and i'm like, "oh my gosh." and i tell her how much i love muhammad ali. And i don't think about it, and the next thing i know, i'm chatting to her husband, jon bon jovi, who i don't know very well but who is a nice person. And i don't think about it. After some time has passed, he adds something to the effect of, "oh yeah, we're meeting muhammad ali tomorrow." i cannot bring myself to admit that i would like speaking with him. I usually respond with something along the lines of, "omg i'm going to die of jealousy right now, that guy is my biggest hero."

After that, i don't give it any more thought, and i go home. Actually, after i drop off jon bon jovi, i walk across the road to visit dónal lunny, and we end up having love, and i end up conceiving my third kid. This shouldn't have occurred since i wasn't even close to halfway through my period; in fact, she was menstruation. However, it did happen. The long-awaited baby boy arrives two weeks early, on the day when his father celebrates his own birthday. This is a kid that was always going to be born, and the name ali is going to be a part of its name. Because it was during this week that i first spoke with ali.

Someone calling themselves muhammad ali's sports agent calls me early on a sunday morning and asks whether my friend jake and i are interested in seeing muhammad ali at the berkeley court hotel. They say they are muhammad ali's agency. Do you know whether or not a bear ever defecates at the vatican? Naturally, we are interested in having a conversation with muhammad ali. After getting my kid out of bed, we got in the car and headed there. As soon as i entered the room, muhammad ali made a kissy face at me, indicating that he wanted me to kiss him. That's enough to make me nervous; all of a sudden, i feel like this stranger may be my biological father. I give him the kiss, and as i do so, i think to myself, "oh my god, i just kissed muhammad ali on the lips." it's evident that he's not being sexual; their interaction is platonic.

Ali, who was already experiencing the latter stages of parkinson's disease at that point, begins to tease jake, which is a really endearing behavior on her part. He gets out of his chair and is able to do a magic trick in which he stands by the entrance and makes it seem as if he is levitating by raising up one of his feet and somehow magically concealing the other. He does this by hiding the other foot behind the lifted foot. Perhaps it floated in midair. In addition to that, he presented me with a wonderful present, which was a compilation of biblical inconsistencies that he himself had compiled into a book. After having some conversation with his wife and children in the next room, it is soon time for us to go. However, just as we are about to leave the room, his representative approaches us and inquires as to whether or not we would be interested in accompanying mr. Ali to the special olympics. The next thing you know, jake and i are riding in an army vehicle with a member of the armed forces. In the end, we were the ones who escorted muhammad ali and sat with him. And we are the only ones who have chosen to sit with him, the only ones who are assisting him through the night.

Obviously, his family is here, but the responsibility for us has been given to mr. Ali. As he travels down the aisle to take his position in croke park waiting for the special olympics to begin, it is necessary for me to assist him in putting on his jacket. As i was putting on his jacket, i was on the verge of crying. He is walking so close behind me that i can hardly see him, and he is unable to button his jacket without my assistance. This is my paternal grandfather. I am assisting my father in putting on his jacket right now. Even just thinking about it makes me want to weep.

Everyone wanted to see mandela, of course, and everyone wanted to meet ali, too, but people separated into battle lines. You were either ali or mandela, while the rest of us were ali.

As we were leaving to take ali back to her vehicle, i saw the second most beautiful sight of my life: the whole catering crew, young and elderly, sobbing, simply crying, because they were so happy to see ali. Since i feel sorry for him, which is something i try very hard to avoid doing since no one should feel sorry for ali. It's possible that his body was impacted, but there was unquestionably nothing wrong with his state of mind. I cannot recall ever having seen anything.

   Amazing in any case, there were people peering out of virtually every single window space and driveway in order to view such a holy guy stroll through the location.
   After that night, I stayed in contact with Ali's agent for a short period of time. I was genuinely quite interested in sleeping with him (I was actually ovulating that week), and I continued in touch with him for a short period of time. But he was fortunate enough to have a buddy stay with him, so it didn't end up happening. I presented him with a ring featuring a Rasta lion.
   Oh, I completely forgot to tell you that. Ali spent some time drawing a stunning picture on a tablecloth during a break in the performance. It seemed like a massive ship navigating across the valley. He sketched a miniature version of one of their battles on the other side of the tablecloth. In the dressing room, the soldier and I glance at each other and say, "You're going to get off"; "No, you're going to sink"; "No, you're going to sink"; "No, you're going to sink." mostly due to the fact that we were debating among ourselves who should receive it. I triumphed without a doubt. Ali signed it for me, and she gave it to me, and I gave it to my son Jake a year ago, since he is now thirty-two years old, and I wanted to wait until he was mature enough to take care of him

before I entrusted him with the responsibility. Ali signed it for me, and she gave it to me.

Everything was enchanted, and I never in a million years would have guessed that it would take place in my life. I have been an extremely fortunate person in that every one of my aspirations has come true at some point in my life. But much more than that, the fantasies I never thought were possible for me to have came true. My third kid would not have been born had it not been for that week, the fact that my son's father lived only down the street, and the grace of God that Ali's sports agent had someone to remain with him while he was in the hospital. My son's name is Nevi'imNesta Ali Shane, and his middle name is Shane. The books of the prophets are referred to by their Hebrew name, Nevi'im. He was aware that he would be raised in a somewhat fatherless household, and because of this, he considered the prophets to be his biological fathers and his masculine role models.

Bob Marley is better known by his birth name, Nesta. Ali, along with Dylan, has been designated to serve as my best man, and Shane stands in the shadow of my good buddy Shane macgowan, a musician. It was a very eventful week, and I have Muhammad Ali to thank for the birth of my kid. I can honestly say that this was the most incredible thing that has ever happened to me in my whole life, with the obvious exception of having children.

LOU REED

The only other time i remember being astonished was when i met lou reed, a guy whose work i didn't know i admired nearly as much as i did until i met him. The song "busload of faith" from his new york album had really captivated me, and as a result, i had played the record quite a bit. And then all of a sudden i find myself at carnegie hall, where i've been asked to perform in roger daltrey's fifty-year-old birthday performance. And back in those days, he was known for his mischievous ways, such as the time he asked random individuals whether he could sing chorus with them.

As a result, i let it be known that, if it were at all feasible, i would adore the opportunity to sing some backup vocals with lou reed. And the next thing i know, lou reed enters into my dressing room and begins chatting to me; i could sense that he felt it was cheeky for me to ask him if he might perform backup vocals. And the next thing i know, he walks out. When i asked him whether he could, all i could see was his lips moving as he said yes. I was having trouble understanding what he was saying; everything poured out all at once like a whirlwind, whirlwind, whirlwind, like if i were on an acid trip. Even though his lips and face were moving, i was unable to make out a single word that he was saying. It was quite similar to experiencing a panic attack. After my boyfriend left the backstage area, i needed to ask my buddy doodles, who was also there, to hold my hand for the next half an hour. I sang background vocals for lou, but i can't even recall which songs i contributed to since at the time i wasn't on earth; rather, i was someplace in the sky. And soon after that, i had a lovely encounter with the same gorgeous guy, which was really unforgettable.

I was asked to perform in a performance in london that was going to be called the white room. The concept behind the show was going to be that six or seven bands would set up in a circle, and each band would play a couple of songs before moving on to the next band in the circle. Since of what i did on saturday night live, everyone turned their backs on me when i arrived at the dress rehearsal since the trend at the time was to treat me as if i were a madman or an outcast as a result of my appearance on snl. It seems that no one, other than the band that i front, is interested in working with me. Despite this, everyone seemed to be as thrilled about lou reed being on the program as i was.

When lou reed attends the dress rehearsal, he makes a point of completely ignoring everyone in the room with the exception of me. He goes to great measures to do this. It makes an effort to locate me, and once it does, it clings to me. He embraces me in a kind manner, as if we are quite familiar with one another. It was a very kind gesture on his part since he didn't have to do that, and it shifted everyone's perspective on how they should respond to me in that environment. While i was completing my performance and practice, i began to get a modicum of respect from others around me. Since that time, mr. Lou reed has had a special place in my heart, and i often find myself thinking about HIM.

SOME LESSONS AND REAL STORIES

More than anything else on this earth, acting is my greatest passion. In addition to my own children, of course. When i think about getting ready to go on another tour (once the epidemic has passed, of course), one of the things that goes through my head is how strange and even dangerous certain celebrities can be.

A long time ago, we had a performance in las vegas; i believe it took place at the hard rock cafe. Johnny depp attended the event, and then he went backstage after the performance. His visit occurred at a period when we had been on tour for so long that we had begun to experience some mental deterioration as a result of the experience.

My cellist, caroline dale, had a bag that was shaped like a plush sheep that was intended for children. The name shaun has been given to the sheep. He had accompanied us on the trip everywhere, and he eventually became our mascot. That evening in las vegas, we came to the conclusion that we should wed this sheep to another stuffed animal that had been passed around among our group. Johnny depp was required to wait nearby and watch us go through this forty minute wedding since it was such an intricate event.

It goes without saying that i never saw him again after that. In point of fact, it is not the case. Recently, i encountered him at the birthday celebration for shane macgowan, who is now sixty, and he said to me, in a very kind manner, that he truly had a great time at that party. I have no doubt that in his mind we seemed insane to him. Whether it was a coincidence or not, all of this took place in las vegas when johnny was filming the movie fear and loathing in las vegas, in which he plays the role of hunter s. Thompson.

In connection with the topic of unusual encounters or not strange experiences, the narrative that i tore up john f. Kennedy jr.'s phone number after he gave it to me at a luxury dinner is completely untrue. The story also claims that i did not meet john f. Kennedy jr. Fantastic narrative, but i've never even had the pleasure of meeting the guy. She is no different from any other woman in that regard; had she met him, she would have been all over him like a monkey. In that case, i must have been homosexual in order to have declined that number.

In addition, there have been certain misunderstandings about anthony kiedis and myself from the band the red hot chili peppers. In his autobiography titled scar tissue, he writes of the two of us locking lips. Never came to pass.

He claims there was some kind of love involvement between us. Just in your head, only.

We used to hang out with, and not only is he a really kind gentlemen, but i also recall him assisting me in transporting my kid to the hospital at one point. When he insisted on going farther, i became agitated. May god be with him. Not because he attempted to kiss me, but because he intimated that he'd want to, you know, sort of fuel the fire, he had o'connor's rage running rampant inside of him, and i could feel it. He was really confused and thought that i was another bull female. That did not occur at any time.

MR BIG THINGS

It's not only the rumors that go about when you meet a celebrity that might be unsettling; there's also the risk that some individuals are eager to injure you for the sake of their own advantage.

Someone who seems to be my friend saw a picture of me on my ipad that i had taken myself, and i immediately emailed my spouse, who has an unusual interest in pocket billiards. I'm wearing nothing but an extremely tiny french maid uniform in it, and my butt is clearly seen.

It's a good thing i hold the rights to the picture, since my so-called buddy handed it to a knucklehead who is now trying to sell it to irish newspapers over the phone. Luckily, i do. Someone i know who is a reporter phoned me to let me know (excuse the pun).

I have made up my mind not to have anything published, so i grab the number of the dumb buddy of mine who is a writer and send him a text message claiming that i am a reporter for an english tabloid and i want to purchase the picture. He finds romantic success. And the three of us came to an agreement that we would meet him at a petrol station around five miles away from my home. I'm going to be there early and i'm going to wear a long brown wig. And during this time, i wait in my car for around twenty minutes until i am able to determine whose vehicle it is in. It seems that he has parked his car just next mine.

I go inside the shop and act as if i'm going to purchase something. And when i'm heading back, i make a point of stopping by his vehicle and taking a photo of his license plate in a very pretentious manner.

He does not understand. Looking at me with a curious expression, as though wondering what this lady is up to. He has it worked out by the time i've gotten back to my vehicle and buckled myself in. And up your pace as you get towards the motorway. In the meanwhile, i give chase in my mother's seven-seater automobile at a rate of roughly three miles per hour. There is a full-fledged automobile pursuit up until the point when he takes a left turn in the vehicle that is going faster. He travels down a rural road and is successful in avoiding capture. He has a lot of local knowledge. It is the location of his home.

I decided to phone him. It seems like he's about to throw up. Please be aware that i am the owner of the copyright. He denies that my so-called buddy was the one who handed it to him and refuses to confess it. However, she is the only one who has used my ipad, therefore it must have been her.

His apology is sincere. So it is written. And he will be the one to take the picture. Never again do i hear anybody mention it to me. And i won't have to worry about running into that so-called buddy ever again. It is not the first time that he has taken advantage of me for financial gain. It fills me with utter despair. He is always taking items that belong to me. Also, other people are doing it. In point of truth, it already does crush my heart but doing so much more so.

JAKE, ROISIN, SHANE AND YESHUA

i have four children by four different fathers, but i have only married one of them. in addition, i have married three other guys, but none of them are the father of my children.

i can state without a shred of doubt that the men who are the fathers of my first and last children are among the closest friends i have anywhere in the world. on the other hand, because we were the parents of the two children who were in the middle, we would always cross the street whenever we saw each other.

as i mentioned earlier, the conception of my first son, jake, came as a very pleasant surprise. a friend of mine had told me that the fourteenth day of one's cycle is the safest, so i waited until then to have sexual relations with jake's father. this event took place in some rural town in england while a madonna concert was being broadcast on television.

i would say that jake suffered a little bit as a result of the fact that i was extremely young when i had him and that i suddenly had great success in the music business: the publication of my debut album was three weeks before he was born. i believe that these two factors contributed to jake's difficulties. when i was twenty years old, i certainly did not have the same level of comprehension of the idea of selflessness that one should have when they become a parent.

when it came to jake and my three other children, i am certain that i was a decent mother; but, it is challenging to be a genuinely good mother when you are a travelling musician. she was kind and kind, but she traveled a lot, and even when she was at home, she seemed like a robot; she was constantly weary and fatigued, and she was also extremely worried that she may turn out to be like my own mother. because of this, i made it a point to always have a babysitter available, as i was terrified that i would become just like her. at the end of the day, jake could have been agitated as a result of this. i believe that it was misunderstood to imply that part of me didn't care, but i wanted to make sure that my children would never have to go through what i went through; if i was in some type of mood, i could go upstairs or out of the home, and my children wouldn't have to deal with it. i wanted to make sure that my children would never have to go through what i went through.

    having jake when he was very little had a number of perks, particularly considering the fact that we were very close friends. we became closer to one another as i got older. although i'm not sure whether it was always a positive thing that we were closer as friends than we were as mother and son, our connection was still incredibly wonderful.

    my children have never been fans of what i have to offer in the kitchen. my cooking skills aren't very excellent. in point of fact, putting it that way is an understatement. you could use whatever i prepare to bring down a house or smash a window. it's that strong. because of this, jake was able to become a skilled cook at a very early age and now works as a head chef at a restaurant in dublin. he has an outstanding work ethic, which is something that makes me extremely proud of him. this young guy puts forth an incredible amount of effort in all he does.

because jake now has two children of his own, a girl named naime and a son named louie, i am now the grandma of two handsome boys who are presently one and three years old. naime and louie were both born to jake.

approximately two or three years ago, when i was ill, it was really challenging for jake to be near me. but i am relieved to report that we are back to being very good friends, and i adore that boy with every fiber of my being, just as i love each and every one of my children. in point of fact, i tell each of them individually that they are my favorite, but i caution them to keep that information to themselves and not share it with their siblings. i make it a point to tell each and every one of them, "you are my best. don't let anybody else know.

roisin, my daughter, was not an unanticipated occurrence; rather, her arrival was deliberate. her father is a journalist by the name of john waters, and he used to work for the irish times, which is a newspaper in ireland. our meeting was arranged so that he could ask me questions regarding my contentious song "famine," which was included on the album universal mother.

i wouldn't say that we fell in love with one other because we didn't. she had recently had a spontaneous abortion. we had a lot of fun together and decided to have a kid with the idea that we would not remain a couple once the child was born. consequently, we were successful in conceiving roisin, and we worked out a plan wherein she would divide her time equally between her father and me. even though i don't have anything to do with john, i can attest to the fact that he is an outstanding and outstandingly lovely parent.

i feel a lot of pride for roisin, particularly due to the fact that she was such a model kid when she was younger; i don't know of any misdeeds that she committed. but if there is one thing i can reveal to you about him, it is that he has a guardian angel. not only have i seen this guardian angel, but several of his friends have also seen this tiny angel. i am not the only one who has seen him.

when her friends informed me that they saw this angel girl, i didn't believe them, and when one of my boyfriends said that he had also seen this redheaded girl, i didn't believe him too. i didn't trust her friends. at least, not until one morning when roisin and i were sharing a bed while i was pregnant with my third child, shane, and we both got up to use the bathroom. when i opened my eyes, the angel was still there, seated atop roisin with her head resting on her hands as if she was bored and waiting for roisin to come to. i observed a girl with red hair who was wearing a hoodie with white and red stripes.

not frightening enough for me to go back asleep again. when i awoke an hour later, the girl was still perched on roisin when i looked over at her. after that, i went back to sleep, and the next time i woke up, the female was no longer there. a week later, though, as i was reprimanding roisin about the condition of her bedroom in what i call the utility room rather than the utility room, a massive bottle of water that held four liters was knocked off the counter and into the floor. nevertheless, it is very evident that the guardian angel was not pleased to learn that i was angry with roisin.

on the day of roisin's second birthday, she came dashing over to the table where a carving knife stood with its pointy edge positioned just in front of her eyes. it is clear that his guardian angel was responsible for the moment the knife lifted into the air and went to the left, away from his face, when he was just millimeters away from it. even though i haven't seen or heard any guardian angels around any of my other children, i still believe in their existence. on the other hand, roisin's guardian angel has such a robust personality that he manifests himself at times.

it's interesting to note that roisin, like jake, also works in the culinary industry; however, roisin specializes in pastry cooking. he received his education in paris and is currently employed in ireland. his hands are really little and delicate. with those tiny fingers of hers, she was always able to construct the smallest of clay animals, and today she crafts gorgeous vegan cakes and sweets.

it's quite amusing to me that two of my boys have turned out to be excellent chefs so far. on the other hand, i've seen that they never give their mother any care packages including food. because i have a moderate form of anorexia, i sometimes think about starving myself. however, i would still want some of the roisin cakes to come in a box, so i'm keeping my fingers crossed that she would send me one when she finishes reading this book.

you should avoid coming into contact with roisin at all costs. and if you want to interact with roisin in any manner, you must first become a fan. roisin will get up and move away from you as soon as she can. if she had her mother's anger, thank heavens, she would have turned her back on you, shut up, and never bothered to talk to you again. she does not have her mother's temper. she has the capacity to walk away from an argument, which is something i appreciate in her because i have a tendency to go right into one. in this regard, i look forward to my daughter as a role model, and i want to one day be just like her.

roisin has found true love and fulfillment in her marriage to a charming guy whom she refers to as poldy. he is an identical replica of roisin's brother jake, who is a really kind person. roisin and jake have always had a wonderful friendship; in fact, they practically sit on one other's knees, embrace, and cuddle. roisin and jake have a wonderful relationship. my guess is that they didn't get into a fight. if you mess with roisin, you're going to have to deal with jake, and believe me when i say that's not something you want to test out. roisin is very protective of jake.

I have four children by four different fathers, but I have only married one of them. Although I have four children, I have never been married. In addition to this, I have wed three other men, but none of them are the biological fathers of my kids.

I can say without a shadow of a doubt that the guys who are the fathers of my first and last children are among the dearest friends I have anywhere in the world. They are also the men who are responsible for the birth of my children. On the other hand, given that we were the parents of the two children who were located in the midst of the group, anytime we saw each other on the street we would always go the other direction.

As I said before, I was taken completely by surprise when I found out that I was going to have my first son, Jake. Because my buddy had informed me that the fourteenth day of one's cycle is the most secure time to engage in sexual activity, I postponed having sexual intercourse with Jake's father until that time. This incident occurred in a little town in England somewhere in the middle of a Madonna performance that was being aired live on television.

I would say that Jake suffered a little bit as a consequence of the fact that I was so young when I had him and that I suddenly had huge success in the music industry: the publishing of my first album was three weeks before he was born. I would say that Jake suffered as a result of the fact that I was quite young when I had him and that I suddenly had such a big success in the music business. I feel that these two aspects were contributors to Jake's predicaments in some way. When I was twenty years old, I definitely did not have the same degree of grasp of the concept of selflessness that one ought to have when they become a parent. When I became a parent, I should have had this level of comprehension.

I have no doubt that I was a wonderful mother to Jake and to my three other children; yet, it is difficult to be a really excellent mother when you are a musician who is always on the road. She was sweet and gentle, but she traveled a lot, and even when she was at home, she seemed like a robot; she was always tired and worn, and she was also really frightened that she may turn out to be like my own mother. She was a robot. Since a result of this, I made it a point to ensure that there was always a babysitter available, since I lived in constant fear that I would turn out just like she did. Jake, at the end of the day, could have experienced agitation as a direct consequence of this. I feel that it was misconstrued to indicate that part of me didn't care, but

I wanted to make sure that my children would never have to go through what I went through; if I was in some kind of mood, I could go upstairs or out of the house, and my children wouldn't have to deal with it. I wanted to make sure that my children would never have to go through what I went through. I didn't want my children to ever have to go through what I had to go through, and I did all in my power to make that happen.

Having Jake around when he was a young child provided a variety of benefits, especially when taking into account the fact that we were very good friends at the time. As I became older, we gravitated toward one another more and more. Our relationship was still very beautiful, despite the fact that I'm not quite certain whether or not it was ever a good thing that we were closer to one another as friends than we were as mother and son.

My children have never been enthusiastic about the meals that I prepare in the kitchen for them. My abilities in the kitchen aren't exactly top-notch. To say it that way is, in point of fact, an underestimate of the situation. You could knock down a house with anything I prepare, or you could shatter a window with it. That's how powerful it is. As a result of this, Jake was able to develop his skills in the kitchen at a very young age, and he now holds the position of head chef at a restaurant in Dublin. He has an exceptional work ethic, which is one of the many reasons why I am so immensely proud of him. This young man gives an exceptionally high degree of effort in all that he does.

Because Jake now has two children of his own, a daughter called Naime and a son named Louie, I am now the grandmother of two gorgeous boys who are now one and three years old. Naime and Louie were both named after Jake's children. Both Naime and Louie were delivered into the world by Jake.

Back about two or three years ago, when I was dealing with a serious illness, it was very difficult for Jake to be in the same room with me. However, I am glad to say that we have resumed our previous status as very close friends, and I cherish that boy with every ounce of my being, just as I loved each and every one of my children. In point of fact, I tell each of them separately that they are the one I love the most, but I warn them not to discuss this knowledge with their other siblings and to keep it to themselves. I make it a point to tell each and every one of them, "You are the finest. I could not have done it without you. Do not reveal this information to anybody else.

My daughter Roisin's coming was not a surprise to me; rather, it was something I had planned for and looked forward to. Her father, who goes by the name John Waters, is a journalist. He once had a position at the Irish Times, which is a daily that is published in Ireland. Our meeting was planned so that he might question me about my controversial song "Famine," which was included on the album Universal Mother. These inquiries were to be directed against me.

To say that we fell in love with one another is not accurate since it did not happen. She had just recently gone through with an unplanned abortion. We had a good time as a couple and made the decision to have a child with the understanding that we would not continue our relationship once the child was born. As a result, we were successful in conceiving Roisin, and we devised a strategy in which she would spend an equal amount of time with both her father and myself. Even though I have nothing to do with John, I can testify to the fact that he is an exceptional and exceptional gorgeous dad. This is despite the fact that I have nothing to do with John.

I have a great deal of pride for Roisin, especially as a result of the fact that she was such a model child when she was younger; I am not aware of any wrongdoings that she did when she was younger. However, if there is one thing about him that I can divulge to you, it is the fact that he has a guardian angel. Not only have I seen this guardian angel, but numerous of his other friends have also reported seeing this angel in its teeny-tiny form. There are others besides myself who have reported seeing him.

I didn't trust her friends when they told me that they had seen this angel girl, and when one of my boyfriends stated that he had also seen this redheaded beauty, I didn't believe him too. I didn't believe anybody who claimed to have seen this girl. I did not have faith in her other pals. At least, not until the morning that Roisin and I were sharing a bed when I was pregnant with my third child, Shane, and we both got up to use the toilet. That was the first time I realized that Roisin and I were sleeping together. The angel was still there when I opened my eyes; she was sat on top of Roisin with her head resting on her hands, as if she was bored and waiting for Roisin to awaken to consciousness. I saw a young lady with auburn hair who was wearing a sweatshirt with horizontal stripes of white and red.

Not terrifying enough to keep me up when I should have been sleeping. After I had been asleep for an hour, I glanced over at Roisin and saw that the female was still sitting on top of her. After that, I went back to sleep, and the next time I woke up, the woman was gone. After that, I went back to sleep. A week later, though, as I was reprimanding Roisin about the state of her bedroom in what I refer to as the utility room rather than the utility room, a big bottle of water that contained four liters was knocked off the counter and into the floor. I was irritated since I had just cleaned her room. Nevertheless, it is quite clear that the Guardian Angel was not happy to discover that I was upset with Roisin. The Guardian Angel's expression reflects this displeasure.

On the day of Roisin's second birthday, she ran hastily over to the table where a carving knife was resting with its sharp edge directed directly into her eyes. When he was just millimeters away from the knife, it suddenly rose into the air and moved to the left, away from his face. It is obvious that his guardian angel was responsible at this event. I continue to have faith in the existence of guardian angels despite the fact that I have never seen nor heard any of them when they were watching after any of my other children. On the other hand, Roisin's guardian angel has such a strong personality that he sometimes makes his presence known to Roisin.

It is noteworthy to notice that Roisin, like Jake, works in the culinary sector; however, Roisin specializes in baking pastries. Jake also works in the food industry. His formal schooling was completed in Paris, and he is now living and working in Ireland. His hands are rather little and delicate in appearance. She has always been able to make the tiniest of clay creatures, and now she crafts stunning vegan cakes and sweets using the same dexterity that allowed her to construct the tiniest of clay animals.

It has been rather humorous for me to see that two of my sons have developed into really skilled cooks so far. On the other hand, it has come to my attention that they never send their mother any care packages that include food. I suffer from a mild type of anorexia, and as a result, I often entertain the idea of starving myself. Despite this, I would still want some of the Roisin cakes to arrive in a box, so I'm keeping my fingers crossed that she will give me one after she is done reading this book. Nevertheless, I do want some of the Roisin cakes to come in a box.

You should do everything in your power to avoid having any kind of interaction with Roisin. In addition, if you wish to communicate with Roisin in any way, the first step is to become a fan of hers. As soon as Roisin is able to do so, she will get up and walk away from you. If she had her mother's fury, thank goodness, she would have walked away from you, kept quiet, and not bothered to speak to you again. She would have turned her back on you. Her anger is nothing like that of her mother's. She is able to disengage herself from a contentious situation, which is a quality that I admire in her since I have a propensity to jump straight into conflict situations. In this respect, I look forward to the opportunity of having my daughter serve as a model for me, and I want to one day be the same as she is.

Roisin's marriage to a dashing man, whom she affectionately refers to as Poldy, has provided her with both real love and satisfaction. He is an indistinguishable twin of Jake, Roisin's brother, who is a really good-natured person. Roisin and Jake have had a beautiful relationship from the beginning of their lives; in fact, they are so close to one another that they almost sit on one another's knees, hug, and snuggle. Roisin and

Jake have an amazing connection with one another. My best guess is that there wasn't a fight between the two of them. Believe me when I say that you do not want to put yourself in that position, because if you mess with Roisin, you will have to deal with Jake, and that is not something you want to try out. Jake is under Roisin's watchful eye the most of the time.

THE WIZARD OF OZ

The reason i have not written much about what happened between the years 1992 and 2015 is because in august 2015, after i had written the first part of this book, i had a radical open surgery hysterectomy in ireland, followed by a complete collapse.

I had gotten as far as the saturday night live tale, but after that, i didn't write anything further for the four years it took me to recover from the accident, and when i did, i couldn't recall much of what it took. Occurred before him. I had gone as far as the saturday night live story.

Because the mental health system in ireland was failing me (for example, they didn't offer me any hormone replacement therapy), and because no one who knew me wanted to have anything to do with me because i was so crazy that everyone was terrified of me, i spent the majority of 2016 and 2017 in various parts of the united states as part of my journey toward recovery. I did this because the mental health system in ireland was failing me, and because no one who knew me wanted to have anything to do with me. No one had ever taken the time to inform either of us that the removal of my ovaries would result in a condition known as surgical menopause, also known as menopause multiplied by ten thousand, and that it was possible for me to become quite unstable as a consequence of this.

In the united states, they will inform your family members these facts, and they will also tell the patient themselves. In the united states, those sent to psychiatric institutions are told that they have completely lost their femininity. In addition to that, they gave you hormone replacement. In ireland, there was none of it to be found. After having my uterus removed in dublin, i was discharged from the hospital with no information, only a bottle of tylenol, and a follow-up appointment that i just could not bring myself to attend.

Because i suffered from persistent endometriosis, i was forced to have surgery. It turned out that i didn't really need having my ovaries removed either. Simply put, the physician came to the conclusion that he "might as well" have them removed. You would have a great deal more knowledge on the years 1992 to 2015 if i had just left them. However, it may be beneficial to forget some things. Being a social pariah for three decades after leaving snl caused a great deal of emotional anguish for him.

That is not something that i would modify in any way. There are certain things that are more important than being accepted by society.

In 2016, when i was traveling around the united states, i stayed for a few days with the one and only person i knew who could have a vacant apartment. After that, he arranged for me to stay with the walkers, a kind and welcoming family he knew. Which made me pleased because i didn't like the way he handled his wife; he treated her as if she was garbage. This made me happy because i didn't like the way he treated his wife. (i should have brought her with me when i went, but i didn't).

During the time that i was living with the walkers, who had a home in the lush chicago suburb of wilmette, i went to quite a few sessions with a psychiatrist and got a great deal of therapy. The drummer for morrissey is named matt walker. Charlotte is the name of his wife. And it is those people who i owe my life to because if it weren't for them forcing me to live with them and if charlotte hadn't stayed with me and taken me to appointments with the therapist and the doctor, i wouldn't be sitting here writing this now. I owe my life to them. At that time, i was unable to walk if i did not have it.

However, all in all, we had a great time. She shares my gloomy sense of humor. His mother, who is ninety years old and has long, black hair, is the most beautiful woman he has ever seen, and she is still with him. When he was young, he had a large number of lovers. And she is quite unfiltered. You two are going to laugh heartily at her jokes. I call her by a slang moniker that is so derogatory that i won't even put it out. However, it used to simultaneously make her laugh and weep. Because of how accurate it was.

However, i had been residing in the walker daughter's room, and since she had just returned from college, it became necessary for me to find my own place to live. I relocated to a hotel in the neighboring town of waukegan.

I had a lot of time to myself. But another thing that i liked about the hotel was that it allowed smoking inside. And i really adored the enormous walmart that was just across the street from the hotel. It was there that i purchased meaningless material items in an effort to experience some kind of feeling and to make my room seem more like it belonged to me.

At some time, i purchased pot that made me feel unwell. As a result, i took the decision to stop using weed and went to a rehabilitation center in san francisco that was suggested to me by someone who knew my therapist. I stayed there for a total of three months. After that, i traveled back to ireland for a week, but nobody there seemed interested in meeting up with me. As a result, i relocated back to the united states, specifically to new jersey, where my boss arranged for me to share an apartment with him. But the want to end my life was so strong that i couldn't remain in this state for more than a day, and i had to keep coming to the hospital to get treatment.

After dozens of visits to hackensack university medical center, and after parting ways with my manager, and after moving into a motel somewhere from new jersey, and after i had a kidney stone and made a video appeal on facebook for someone to come help me, i got a call in the dr. Phil ward on the last of my three visits to englewood hospital. These visits came after i had made dozens of visits to hackensack university medical center. I'm starting to wonder whether this may be my cinderella moment.

He is willing to provide a hand to me. He claims that his investigator tracked me out via my immigration attorney michael wildes, citing the fact that his image and name had been posted on my facebook page.

As phil presents himself to me over the phone, i am being supervised by an emt who is perhaps eighteen years old, blonde, and has the palest complexion one can imagine. This is standard procedure for all suicidal patients. I've never been in an american hospital when one wonderful woman wasn't with me all day and another one all night. It was those women who inspired me to become a medical assistant since chatting and joking with them was more therapeutic than any drug or treatment i've ever had. Knowing that they would be there even as i slept gave me the feeling of being a mother for the first time in my life. Therefore, it was not suffocating to witness; rather, it was loving.

Anyway, her skin was so pale that it looked like paper, so when this wicked mad lady went by and spilled half a cup of boiling tea on the girl's arm and no one rushed to assist her, i felt like i had no choice but to hang up the phone. No one came to help the girl after the woman dropped the tea on her arm. While i was making a scene at the front desk because she had been neglected, a nurse handed me a letter in the midst of the commotion. It comes from the individual who served as my physician in hackensack. He is familiar with dr. Phil and agrees with the physician from englewood that participating in the show would be detrimental to one's health.

Both of them are completely insane in my opinion. He is channeling his inner dr. Phil. He can make anybody better. And they have no clue either, to put it another way! Therefore, what do i have to lose by trying?

Of course, i am the one with the mental illness. But, unfortunately, legally they are unable to prevent me from leaving the hospital (which would have been for the best for me), and i insist on receiving phil's call, which arrives around 10 minutes after the elderly woman spills the tea.

It is essential that you comprehend how badly you want a smoke after spending a few days and nights in any american psychiatric hospital, as this will help you better prepare for your stay there. It's not like ireland, where the sole perk is that they allow you light up. Here, the whole country stinks. In the united states of america, your only option is to use a nicotine patch. Additionally, there is no access to the outdoors. After a week, you start to lose your mind even more than you already were, which is why i insisted on giving up all reason and going to see dr. Phil, which was partly motivated by the fact that i wanted to go out and smoke. In addition to that, he is a casual pot smoker. Which was also excruciatingly painful to be lacking at the moment. Phil was proposing to take me on a journey of eight hours to a rehabilitation facility in the southern united states that he had suggested to some of his other clients. My clever, drug-addled mind realized it was probably hours of smoking pot and cigarettes. And, sure, sir, that was the case all the way through.

While I was in the hospital, a new manager was brought to my attention, and together we went with the driver and a video crew of two people. After Phil had sent the marijuana guy to my vacant apartment to meet with me, I got into the huge black van, kissed Phil, and drove away. He waved his farewell to the manager and then set off into the night, believing that this time he would be able to overcome his illness. I don't mean smoking; I mean being irrationally furious, having suicidal thoughts, and being in so much agony that you can't function outside of a medical facility. I had been hoping that God would intervene on my behalf in the shape of a person so that I may get some assistance. In addition, I was under the impression that God had sent someone by the name of Dr. Phil. I had the impression that he was the actual solution to all of my problems. However, he ought to have been aware that he was batting for the other side. Because he lacked integrity in his spiritual life. On the Jimmy Fallon program, he was questioned about how he and I came to be together. "She reached out to me," he said with me. That is not the case. Jimmy could have been able to accuse him of taking advantage of someone when she was in a vulnerable state if he had been truthful.

So after a total of eight hours of driving, smoking, and conversing, we finally made it to this trauma treatment institution that is perched on the picturesque edge of nowhere. Because of how fragile I was, the medical professionals in New Jersey had warned me that undergoing trauma therapy may be risky. It turned out that they were right. However, no one had paid attention. The first piece of bad news is that several individuals in downtown want to steal my ipad. They may as well have attempted to suffocate me with their attempts to remove my lungs. In the middle of night, I raced all over the property, then I shoved her into my trousers and hid in the bushes as two ladies searched the grounds for me and her on a golf cart. I had to get away from them before they found us. In the end, I caved in, which allowed them to succeed. In addition, as a kind of protest, I refused to take any of my belongings back to my room. I told them that they could have everything they wanted from me as long as they took my ipad. Because it is inhumane to just take away a person's cane and force them to spend all twenty-four hours of every day sitting in their filth with no comfort or entertainment options. Especially in the event that his sh*t turns out to be a significant amount of stress.

Overnight, I changed from feeling some degree of comfort to having no comfort at all. And because of it, I disliked the females. However, this is just for one day. Simply because it turned out that each of them had a charming personality.

As I am walking back to my room from the garden, I run into the psychiatrist who was waiting for me in the trunk of his vehicle. He extends an offer of a fig bar to me. Why, in the name of everything that is holy, would a rocker desire a fig bar? Are you even more insane than I am? I respond by saying that fig bars are more popular with hippies and not with me. It's clear that we won't get along with each other at all.

When everything is prepared for the night, it is already late in the day. Around one in the morning, I make my way to bed. Because appearing on the broadcast was a requirement for Phil to fulfill his obligation to assist me, the crew from Dr. Phil's program will pay a visit first thing in the morning. And I was required to complete it before I could start getting treatments at the facility that had been recommended to me. This way, he won't be able to whine in front of the camera about how horribly he's been taken advantage of and how irresponsible the alleged medical treatment he received at the establishment he advises appears to be.

I mean, to put that into perspective, I am not even certain that any member of my treatment team has accessed any of my medical records at any of the hospitals that I have visited. Including Englewood, which was the neighborhood from where he had abducted me. They didn't seem to be able to answer the question of whether or not I should participate in individual trauma treatment for even one hour per week, much alone for nine hours per day. It felt like a severe beating. Making my condition much more severe.

Anyway, at this point I'm sitting here opposite Dr. Phil, getting ready to record the program. Brimming with aspirations and wishes. The very first thing he says is that he's here because many of my followers contacted him through Facebook after seeing my video and requested him to assist me. He is showing me a big folder that, according to him, is jam-packed with sent demands. Everyone was overflowing with love and support for me. I would want to know whether I am able to preserve the folder along with its contents. He affirms that he will, yet he fails to hand it up to me. It tells me how fortunate I am right now, and that because the location I am in is so luxurious, among other things, it must be the very finest.

He forces me to give him my narrative while the camera is rolling. Because I am weak, I am willing to put my faith in him. And I intend to continue living. So I'm just going to come clean about everything now. I sob like a little child. Even with my mother, he makes me speak to her. The things that "little Sinéad" may desire to express to the world. What ought I to do? Because I believe it is beneficial to me. Oh, and there's also the fact that I get the impression, just before filming starts, that being on the program when I'm in such a delicate state is "courageous" and "will assist others." He then continues on to discuss about a fantastic producer he is familiar with. He assures me that this other person is going to contact me, and that we are going to produce some albums together. He informs me that he just went to a meeting where Steve Bannon was present as we are recording a final stroll around the property where we are shooting. And that at that discussion, individuals associated with Trump really discussed the possibility of MAGA being shortened to MAWA. Bring back the original color of America. When he informed me about it, he seemed quite repulsed.

But I felt that if he was really that furious, he would let everyone know about it. That would be the essence of spiritual integrity. To put everything at danger in order to protect those who are helpless, to run the risk of being labeled insane and of becoming an outcast. No. I didn't have the guts to do it.

After that, I never did see him again since he took off in his helicopter.

The next day, I had a dispute with the psychiatrist that I had been seeing. Because I had neglected to log out before going to smoke, he made the baseless accusation that I was trying to be pampered in order to act like a rock star.

They made fun of me because I would never genuinely want to be treated any differently than anybody else at a rehabilitation facility and they made fun of me for that. And he demonstrated to me how his fig bars had made their way into his head.

I experienced pain. However, I did not utter a single word. I made my way back to my room in a collected manner after leaving his office.

It would seem that he had the incorrect assumption that I was angry, since he rushed up the hill to get away in case I gave pursuit. That didn't make me furious before, but it did make me angry after the fact. You are not allowed to weep in the same room as the fig-eating wimp that is your psychiatrist because he will break down. The psychiatrist is a fig-eater. The Lord Jesus Christ. I warned them that they should never put us in the same room together again out of concern that I might assault him. After that, Phil was the one who got in touch with me. I shared with him my worries over the fig-eater as well as the attention of the other members of the crew. I also let him know that I didn't believe he could help me, which is something that I still believe.

"I don't fail," Dr. Phil is quoted as saying. In addition, he cautioned me from acting inappropriately toward the doctor.

Every time I file an official grievance against a member of the facility's staff, the situation becomes even more precarious. Or about the other suicidal girl that Phil sent them after a concert, who was crying because she did not receive the attention she thought she needed even though she indicated she had wants to end her life. After some time, I was taken out of the main facility and assigned to live by myself in a huge, unoccupied home that was located on the grounds of the institution. It is very forbidden for me to enter the main home. Which infuriates me to the extreme. Such is the nine hours of trauma counseling that are completed each day. (One day, in the midst of a lengthy session of trauma treatment, a member of the staff who is responsible for legal and financial matters steps in. He gave me a copy of the contract that he wanted me to sign and handed it to me. To the effect that if I recorded anything, all other customers would do the same).as a component of your therapy, the music therapist will work with you to create recordings, which will then become the property of the treatment facility. It goes without saying that I did not sign, and it is revolting for someone to go into someone else's therapy session for any reason; it is even more revolting to let that person know that you intended to take advantage of them.)

I eventually go crazy one night, start yelling all over the place, and someone calls the cops on me because i've indicated that I'm considering ending my life. They send me to the nearest hospital, where the doctors determine that I am not really suicidal but more traumatized rather than suicidal. They strongly recommend that I do not go back to the treatment institution. And the officers, out of their kindness, locate a hotel for me and drive me there.

In the morning, I look inside my backpack and discover the key to the large home in which I resided by myself while I was in the rehabilitation facility. And then for some reason chooses to do it again. I give the lone person who drives a cab in town a call. He claims that he was shot in the head during the Korean War, and that all of the women in this town are infatuated with him because of it. As we continue to go down this road, I look to my left and see a beautiful cemetery. Sculptures and sculptures made of white stone. Every single one of the enormous religious symbols and flowers.

There is something that looks like a graveyard for animals off to the right of the road as you are facing this one. There may be a hundred dark stones on the ground, each about the size of a grapefruit, yet there are no graves that can be seen. The grounds are filthy, and the grass has not been trimmed in some time. I inquire with my driver whether it is a cemetery for animals, but he does not respond. "That's for blacks, but I don't hang out with them very much." I can almost feel my heart splitting in two. And now I get why the one and only black woman who works downtown was so taken aback that she opted to weep on her coworker's shoulder when things became too difficult. When it occurred the first time, he was taken aback, and he expressed his gratitude to me as if I had been honored.

When I go to hand in the key, however, they talk me into going to a different rehabilitation facility in Los Angeles instead. To which I agree, and they drive me there before abandoning me. Although I do not know anything about Phil, I have been informed that he is the one who is paying for my stay. After being there for three weeks, I was informed by a member of the staff who was in a foul mood that the center in reality does not have anything to offer me and that what I was told at the first installation was not accurate. There are no unexpected developments there. After that, I go on the road. Since then, I have not had a single communication from any of them.

In 2018, I composed a song that was inspired by all of this. Although there is currently a sample of it available on youtube, the song will be titled "Milestones" and it will be included on my next album. And you are correct; there is no mention of the fig bars.

FORWARD AND NOW

We believe that it is always night in the sky, as this is the belief of islam. I certainly do. And if there is a heaven, i pray that i be allowed to enter there (in case there is a scenario in which i am not allowed to enter). It is difficult for me to accept the idea that god is a harsh being. In the event that i do not earn the blessing, however, i pray that the fact that i have sung may minimize the severity of my many transgressions, which are both nasty and many.

I am quite fond of the flame. I really pray that there are flames in the clouds. When i am unable to be strong on my own, fire helps me.

In addition to this, nighttime is my favorite time since that's when the fire can be enjoyed. And if my evening does not have a fire, nor does my gloomy morning? I am empty within. To the bone, even. I shudder to think what life would be like if i didn't wear my hijab.

When i got back in october of 2018, i started using it again (it is not the same, and yes, i have cleaned it so that my head does not smell on foot). I have been wearing it ever since. We say that islam is at home because it has a comfortable feeling. As a person who had been interested in theology ever since i was a youngster, i found that this was the case for me. Similar like returning home. I spent my whole life looking, through every song and every book, but for some reason, i put off looking into islam till the end. In spite of the fact that i played the call to prayer before each concert for years, i never took the time to really learn it.

I have a pastime that i haven't disclosed to anybody yet. I paint scenes from the bible. It's something i've been doing for a very long time. I normally do, but recently i haven't been since i've realized that practically every person with whom i get into an argument after giving them one ends up being an exception to the rule.

When it is finally time for me to leave this mortal coil, i want all of the people who i have given a painting to to join together in one location and have an exhibition. These two parties had never interacted before. They come from a wide variety of backgrounds. If they haven't messed with the artwork, i'd want for them to have a conversation. And even if they have done so already.

Because each painting took me a month to complete, and because i ended up in the hospital because i wasn't eating, i decided to move to sketching. It was almost like an obsession to paint. These days i draw using markers. And paint made of gold leaf. Easier.the same outcome. This is a kind of prayer for me. Then, throughout the month of october, i found myself sitting down in the middle of the night to paint the call to prayer. It's almost like singing when you pray in another language. It is necessary for you to be aware of what you are saying. Consequently, i was in possession of both the english and arabic copies, and i intended to paint the arabic one. I was so astounded by what "there is no god but god" meant, how it felt in my lips to pronounce it, and the mathematics of it. The phrase "la ilaha illallah" means "there is no god but god." that settled it; i'd arrived at my destination. Because of the beautiful and profound language of the call to prayer, i decided to start reading the qur'an. I was inside the building. I did not become aware of the fact that i had been a muslim until much later in my life. The song "the call to prayer" is the song with the highest level of mathematical intelligence ever created.

Idolatry may be defined as the affection for anything or anybody other than god that a person loves so intensely that they believe they cannot live without it. Or would you rather perish in oblivion without it? It might be a person, it could be a location, or it could be anything. You won't understand unless god chooses to reveal it to you first. Nevertheless, demonstrate to him that he will. A golden calf that is uniquely yours. And this will come as a surprise to you since you believed you embodied the definition of a real believer.

In heaven, people often refer to the location as paradise. Paradise by moonlight.unruffled and unruffled. The gardens are surrounded by rivers that run underneath them. I long for it. Therefore, i subject myself to it every evening in the comfort of my own living room. An blaze. And the shadows, if it weren't for her... Without a doubt, when i think of paradise, i see a beautiful garden. One in which the climate is ideal and in which, despite the fact that you pass by a great number of people, you are not required to show your face if you want not to.

Despite the fact that i really want to, i. To come into view. They have never witnessed me in person. Not even for me to consider. I want to sing in an environment where i can get away with it without god, my grandma, or my mother being angry with me. I am the source of a great deal of unease on this planet. Take after me and try to live a good life.

Singing is the only spiritual activity i've ever engaged in during my whole life. Only the music industry has so much profanity. After a time, tensions begin to arise between them. Because you are in the incorrect setting, you simply are unable to do quality work. The rockabilly club is the kind of place where acid just doesn't cut it. My personality is not suited for a career in the music industry. Not for much of anything at all. In addition to writing songs and performing them in their own right. What's the matter, my dear? I mean acting in general. Born with the talent. I agree, sir.

Do people sing in heaven? That's a question i've always wanted to know. And utter them to those who create the music of the earth? What am i getting at here? The qur'an may be compared to a song. And it was gabriel who brought it to muhammad's attention, having first heard it from gabriel. It was finished after a period of twenty-one years. Actually, god is an excellent musician and songwriter.

I pray that it's true that god is a fan of a good singer. And i'm sure muhammad was blessed with a wonderful singing voice. I really hope that you haven't stopped singing since you arrived in the night paradise. Perhaps if i am calm and still, someone will talk to me.

Printed in Great Britain
by Amazon

8cb488d7-44b4-438d-89a9-74c1a2a35bd6R01